Prais

"We're moving towards times of greater and faster transitions and challenges. I love what you say in Innovation Starts With I—the same applies to leadership."

- Arianna Huffington
Co-Founder, The Huffington Post | Founder and CEO, Thrive Global

"This beautiful book contains wisdom and magic on every page. When you're ready to take the next step, it's here for you."

- Seth Godin
Founder, AltMBA | Author, *This is Marketing*

"This book is filled with vivid images and insights to spark ideas. It might just help you see the world—and yourself—differently."

- Adam Grant
#1 New York Times Bestselling Author, *Think Again* | Host of the TED podcast, *WorkLife*

"At first glance, you might feel you know this topic. But just a few pages in, you'll realize Professor Vellani brings an original view to innovation: authenticity, originality, hybridpreneurship, and more. I either learned or felt validated by her concepts page by page."

- Bracken Darrell
CEO, Logitech

"This book is both visually compelling and intellectually captivating. Let the images and ideas sink in. They will change how you lead."

- Daniel H. Pink
#1 New York Times Bestselling Author,
When, Drive, and *To Sell Is Human*

"No time in history has the entire world experienced a common paradigm shift in how we connect, learn, work, and live. The end of a global pandemic also marked a new beginning for individuals, organizations, and communities. Reinventing oneself is a critical new skill to have in a post-pandemic world. This book beautifully introduces new frameworks designed to help us reimagine our lives in a new normal. The I, We, World concept in the Ripple Impact Framework is a powerful way to assess our capabilities as we design a more meaningful life."

- Farouk Dey
Vice Provost for Integrative Learning and Life Design,
Johns Hopkins University

"Reflecting on your life's journey and preparing you to pivot towards your personal genius is what this book promises."

- Shamini Dhana
Founder and CEO, Dhana Inc.

"Innovation Starts With I captures both energizing inspiration and practical guidance from so many insightful, innovative leaders—including Saleema Vellani. It is a valuable guide for those of us who deeply believe innovation and entrepreneurship are among our most powerful tools for a better future."

- Doug Galen
Co-Founder and CEO, Rippleworks Foundation

"In our fast paced, uncertain, and constantly changing world, it is key to reinvent yourself. Saleema teaches what she has successfully demonstrated multiple times."

- Shelmina Abji
Former Vice President, IBM

"From scheduling 100 coffee meetings to becoming a "hybridpreneur," this thought-provoking book is filled with non-obvious suggestions for how to creatively upend your life and rewrite your career to find more joy in everything you do."

- Rohit Bhargava
#1 Wall Street Journal Bestselling Author and Founder, Non-Obvious Company

"Innovation is driven by an ecosystem of ideas, perspectives, successes, and failures. Vellani brings together learnings from top leaders so that you can tap into a wealth of experiences to forge your own innovations. By reading this book, you'll be inspired to take innovation to the next level and to create impact in new ways."

- Kristy Wallace
CEO, Ellevate

"This book will create ripples in our lives! The magical art and science of storytelling was beautifully woven into the tapestry and fabric of this book. Authenticity and humanity was prevalent throughout. The insights were well-structured and articulated in a memorable way. It was absolutely wonderful to see critical human issues like trust, ethics, values, and empathy highlighted as we propel relentlessly into our exponential future. This is a must read and is destined to be a bestseller!"

- Tariq Qureishy
Futurist | CEO, Xponential and MAD Group

SALEEMA VELLANI

INNOVATION STARTS WITH I

INCREASE YOUR INFLUENCE. IGNITE YOUR IMPACT.

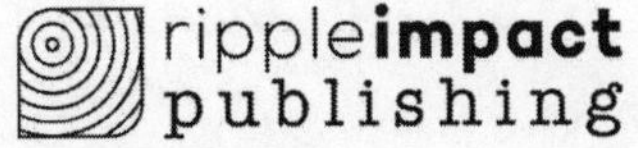

Published in the United States by Ripple Impact Publishing.
rippleimpact.co

Book team appears on Page 275.

ISBN 9781737848509 (paperback)
ISBN 9781737848516 (hardback)
ISBN 9781737848523 (epub)

PRINTED IN THE UNITED STATES OF AMERICA

1 2 3 4 5 6 7 8 9 10

First Edition

This book is dedicated to my late mother,
Mumtaz Remtulla Vellani, an entrepreneur and educator who touched the lives of many.

Through her Montessori school and beyond, she sparked curiosity, spread kindness, brought laughter, and exemplified resilience.

She had big dreams, and through this book, I hope to continue her legacy.

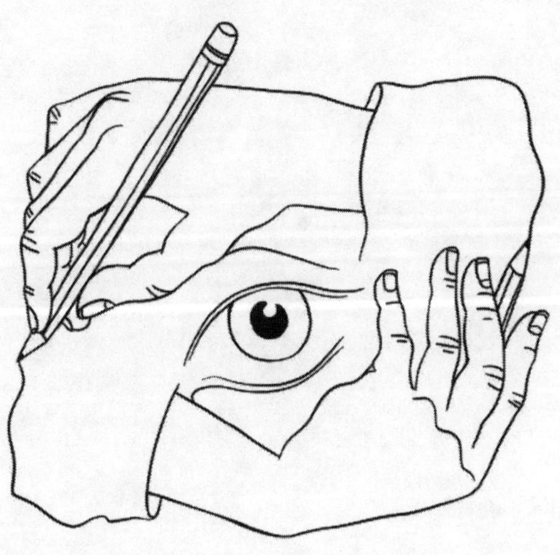

TABLE OF CONTENTS

Innovation Starts With I

I WE WORLD

Chapter 1

Chapter 2

Chapter 3

Chapter 4

I WE WORLD

Chapter 5

Chapter 6

Chapter 7

Chapter 8

I WE WORLD

Chapter 9

Chapter 10

Chapter 11

Chapter 12

The End

Preface

Dear Reader,

My grandfathers were from Gujarat, India, where entrepreneurship is almost a religion and where people are quite nomadic in pursuit of economic opportunities. One day, they took a boat to East Africa, and my parents were born and raised in Tanzania.

In 1972, my mum and dad fled due to political turmoil and nationalization. On a round-the-world air ticket (ah, the good old days), they stopped over in the United Kingdom, and a few months later arrived in Canada with only $100, just in time for my older brother's birth.

My parents, like many immigrants, worked hard to make ends meet. My dad pumped gas and worked in a factory before getting a job at a bank. My mum was a typist and babysat kids in the community. When I was born, she started her own Montessori preschool from home so she could take care of me, even though she only had a high school diploma.

My mom passed away when I was sixteen and my entire life changed. I didn't know how to deal with her being gone. My definition of "home" was shattered. The world seemed unreal. I was relieved that she was no longer suffering, but I was also in shock. How would I live without her?

Her losing battle with cancer forced me to become emotionally independent at a young age. I never asked for help or support. As I embarked on a journey to re-find "home," I landed on a path of entrepreneurship that forced me to reinvent myself several times over.

Many people see me today and think I come from a privileged background. And I'm flattered by that because it means I've shown up. But the truth is, I've had to go through a lot to get to where I am. Just like you've had to go through your own journey.

We often underestimate the highs and lows we face while running a company until we experience it. Lack of grit and inability to adapt are among the main reasons most entrepreneurs fail. Developing the 12 Future-Proof Capabilities I describe in this book has helped me better handle challenging situations. It has helped me innovate myself as I innovated in each company I led or contributed to.

What I've learned along the way is that I love helping others. And I hope this book helps you, in some small way, make your mark on the world.

Please let me know your thoughts.

saleema vellani

INNOVATION ISN'T JUST ABOUT TECHNOLOGY

IT'S ABOUT BEING HUMAN

Introduction

Innovation Re-Envisioned

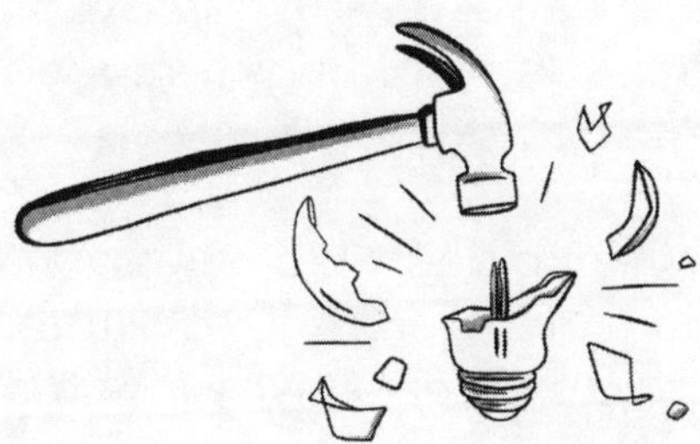

My building was on fire.

Smoke was pouring out of the windows and the roof. Fire engines, sirens blaring, were out front. My neighbors were standing on the sidewalk, being interviewed by the press. The Red Cross was handing out blankets and care packages. I kept blinking. But nothing changed. My house was literally burning down.

After things were safe, the firefighters accompanied us back inside in small groups. There was no electricity. We had to wade through pools of water, and my feet got soaked through my boots.

The fire was the last straw in a year full of rotten straw. I had already lost two jobs. I had gotten divorced, been dumped by two boyfriends, and been rejected by the man I thought was my soulmate. I had temporarily moved into my parents' home due to lack of income. I was going through what I would later learn is called a "lifequake," an involuntary and unavoidable change that happens three to five times in one's life.[1]

My life had been so stable a few months prior. Now it was like I had fallen into a black hole, and couldn't get out. One of the guys who had dumped me said, "You'll find it hard to believe right now, but one day you'll see this is all a blessing in disguise."

He was right. I didn't believe him. Ironically, I was scheduled to attend an intensive two-day life purpose workshop starting the day after the fire. If I might have skipped it before, there was nothing else to do now. So I went.

At the workshop, we dug deep into our psyches and stared at ourselves in mirrors. The workshop facilitator, Paula Recimil, said: "Fire represents change. Maybe it's time you did something different."

Something different? Sure. Anything! But what?

Shortly after the workshop, I got an email from my building saying that I'd be displaced for nine months. Change, huh?

I had recently booked a ticket to India to attend a friend's wedding. I was thinking about canceling, but then I figured I might as well make it an Eat, Pray, Self-love trip and added Thailand and Bali to the itinerary. I packed a few clothes and a book called *Autobiography of a Yogi*. To save money I had organized a one-way ticket—coincidence? I knew I could figure things out while in Asia.

So I embarked on an accidental transformative spiritual journey. What better place than India for that? I visited ashrams, did ayurveda, yoga, and meditation, spent time alone and in group healings, and tried new experiences to find myself. It took three weeks to reach my first epiphany. There I was, sitting in a boat in the backwaters of Kerala, watching a mother wash her baby, when I realized suddenly and with great surprise, I had learned. . .nothing.

All the navel-gazing was doing no good. I was asking more questions and answering none. I had never had a problem answering questions before. What was going on?

I had never asked myself *these* questions before. I had spent my whole life checking boxes based on my perceived definitions of success while steadily "climbing the ladder." I realized my lifequake was a good thing, not a problem. It was time to reinvent myself. The signs had been showing up for some time, but I couldn't hear them, so they got louder and bigger until they brought me to this river, where I suddenly felt I was nobody, and knew nothing.

In yet another "coincidence," my brother started telling me it was time for me to come home and sort my life out. I finally decided to listen to him and start over from someplace familiar.

Innovating In The Reinvention Revolution

Innovation isn't just about technology. It's about being human.

I had no idea that at the same time I was in India, the World Economic Forum was busy defining the Fourth Industrial Revolution.

"The Fourth Industrial Revolution represents a fundamental change in the way we live, work and relate to one another. It is a new chapter in human development, enabled by extraordinary technology advances commensurate with those of the first, second and third industrial revolutions. These advances are merging the physical, digital and biological worlds in ways that create both huge promise and potential peril. The speed, breadth and depth of this revolution is forcing us to rethink how countries develop, how organisations create value and even what it means to be human. The Fourth Industrial Revolution is about more than just technology-driven change; it is an opportunity to help everyone, including leaders, policy-makers and people from all income groups and nations, to harness converging technologies in order to create an inclusive, human-centred future. The real opportunity is to look beyond technology, and find ways to give the greatest number of people the ability to positively impact their families, organisations and communities."[2]

At the time, I wasn't interested in innovating on a global level. I was laser-focused on trying to innovate myself. I was engaging in what I would come to call **The Reinvention Revolution.**

The World Economic Forum was talking about reinventing the world. Later, when I heard about that meeting and its outcomes, my first thought was that in order to innovate on a global level, we have to start with innovating on an individual level.

Innovation starts with "I." It begins with reinventing ourselves. And in the Reinvention Revolution, we need to reinvent ourselves faster and more frequently than ever before.

I had thought of "innovation" as the final output, product, or invention of the creative process. But after realizing the need to go through my own reinvention, I understood that innovation is actually about the *input* that inspires and ignites that process. Innovation starts with knowing who we are and leveraging our unique strengths to make our biggest impact.

We need to be more proactive when it comes to reinventing ourselves, instead of being reactive. And so I wrote this book.

This book takes you through my journey and the steps I went through to reinvent myself, first for myself, then for those close to me, and finally for the world. And although innovation starts with "I," it is executed with others. In retrospect, any time I tried to launch a business or project on my own, I failed. By working with partners, building teams, creating a support network, and engaging with our community, we can better innovate and have a ripple impact on our world.

By innovating from within ourselves, we are able to thrive on an individual level, have a bigger impact on those around us, and better address the world's complex challenges. That's how I came up with **The Ripple Impact Framework** of I, WE, WORLD.

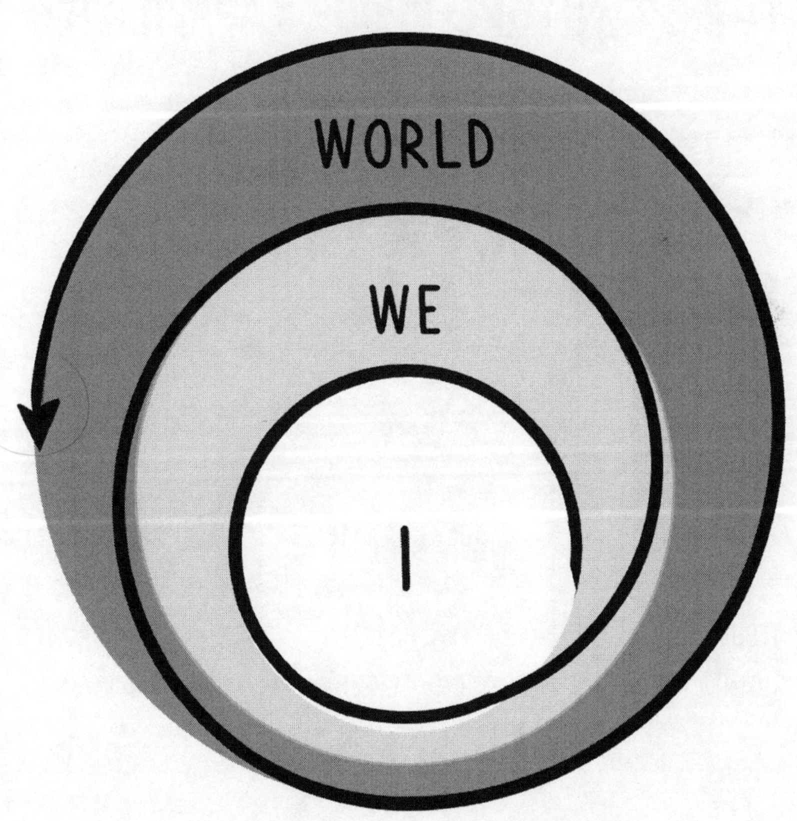

The 12 Future-Proof Capabilities

Innovation starts with I, happens with WE, and has a ripple impact on the WORLD.

Through interviews, workshops, and my own introspection, I realized there are **12 Future-Proof Capabilities** that can be broken down into the Ripple Impact Framework of I, WE, and WORLD.

THE 12 FUTURE-PROOF CAPABILITIES

I

SELF-AWARENESS
CURIOSITY
INTUITION
ORIGINALITY

WE

COLLABORATION
EMPATHY
AUTHENTICITY
STORYTELLING

WORLD

PRIORITIZATION
ADAPTABILITY
GLOBAL MINDSET
INFLUENCE

Within each of the twelve capabilities, what I expected to be the case was not. In some cases, what I needed to develop that capability was exactly the opposite of what I thought I needed to do, or what I had been taught. In other words, I learned this all reactively, by trial and error. But you can use the lessons to be proactive and avoid having an unnecessary lifequake yourself.

By mastering the 12 Future-Proof Capabilities, I became better at doing work that matters while maximizing my impact in this fast-evolving world.

How To Read This Book

The only person stopping you from unleashing your impact is you.

Are you ready for a journey of self-discovery? This book will take you through the stages you need to future-proof yourself.

In "**I**," you'll ignite the spark of innovation within yourself and embark on a reinvention journey.

In "**WE**," you'll learn how to successfully execute innovation by building influence authentically through human relationships.

In "**WORLD**," you'll learn how to scale your vision globally and experience a ripple impact from the initial reinvention journey.

Each part contains four chapters, and each chapter covers one of the 12 Future-Proof Capabilities. Each chapter contains tools that build on the chapters before, so please read the book in order the first time. After that, you can go back and use the topics as a reference.

I've incorporated insights from business leaders, entrepreneurs, thinkers, and students that you will find useful. Each chapter concludes with a collection of some of my favorite relevant quotes.

By following the tools in this book, you can use the principles of future-proofing and innovation to drive your personal growth. And then, in turn, the reinvented you can drive economic growth for yourself, others, and the entire world.

Have fun!

"IF INNOVATION WAS A COCKTAIL, IT WOULD BE A MIX OF VALUES AND LESSONS LEARNED ALONG THE WAY INFUSED WITH A GOOD DOSE OF COURAGE AND THE WILLINGNESS TO BE VULNERABLE."
- VALENTINA NESCI
DIVERSITY + INCLUSION LEADER + CAREER COACH, GOOGLE

"THE *emotional* SIDE OF **INNOVATION** NEEDS TO CHANGE BEFORE AN INDIVIDUAL CAN INNOVATE. WE'RE ON THE VERGE OF **INNOVATION PSYCHOLOGY** AND THAT'S ABOUT TO CRACK OPEN."
– BILL O'CONNOR, INNOVATION STRATEGIST

"WE SEE A BIG BLOW ON THE MARKETING SIDE OF WHAT *AI* IS, BUT VERY LITTLE IS HAPPENING THAT ACTUALLY CHANGES THE WORLD. WE'RE STILL AT THE BEGINNING OF ALL THE **possibilities** OF WHAT CAN BE DONE, CHANGED, AND PUT INTO OPERATION."
– EVA-MARIE MULLER-STULER, CHIEF DATA SCIENTIST, IBM

"PEOPLE MAKE THE MISTAKE THAT **innovation** IS ABOUT **RADICAL** NEW IDEAS, BUT IT'S ABOUT ITERATIVE STEPS."
- ZAC GITTENS, BUSINESS STRATEGIST + STARTUP MENTOR

"**THE PEOPLE WHO** *understand people* **ALWAYS WIN.**"
– ROHIT BHARGAVA
TREND CURATOR + ENTREPRENEUR + AUTHOR

"INNOVATION IS ABOUT TAKING *something old* **AND MAKING THE VISION YOUR OWN.** TAKING AN OLD CONCEPT AND MAKING IT **relevant.**"
- NINA ANSARY, AUTHOR + HISTORIAN

"THE MOST IMPORTANT **INNOVATION** YOU CAN EVER MAKE IS TO INNOVATE **YOURSELF.** AND NOT JUST ONCE."
- MICHAEL LEE
INNOVATION STRATEGIST

"EVERYONE SHOULD WORK TOWARDS BECOMING AN entrepreneur AND LEVERAGE JOBS TO LEARN THE SKILLS WE NEED TO GET TO THAT POINT." - MIKE DUKE
FORMER CHIEF INNOVATION ARCHITECT, WELLS FARGO

"INNOVATION ISN'T ~~DISRUPTION~~. IT'S CHANGING SOMETHING IN SOME AREA OF SOCIETY OR REGION. IT'S NOT CREATING THE NEW FACEBOOK OR GOOGLE. INNOVATION IS SOMETHING THAT WE **DO A LOT MORE THAN WE BELIEVE WE DO.**"
- DIEGO NORIEGA, ENTREPRENEUR + AUTHOR

I

In this section:

- You'll embark on a personal reinvention journey and explore within yourself.
- You'll understand yourself through the lens of those around you.
- You'll develop your gifts and overcome your blind spots using your intuition.
- You'll get comfortable with being uncomfortable to help you evolve into the next version of yourself.
- You'll gain tools to position yourself for the WE part of your reinvention journey.

WARNING: You'll have lots of tools for every step of the way. Be sure to go at your own pace and take breaks.

INNOVATION STARTS WITH
GOING INWARD

Chapter 1

Introspective Exploration

Leaning In To Who I Am

I could feel my heart beating through the silence. Two officials in navy blue uniforms moved back and forth as the waiting area around me filled up with other travelers.

I was at the international airport in Toronto, my hometown, waiting for U.S. Customs and Immigration to let me fly to Washington, D.C. I had just returned from my Eat, Pray, Self-love trip to India, Thailand, and Bali and was ready to move on to my next chapter.

The immigration officer handling my case finally called my name. His nametag said Mario. He flipped through my application paperwork for a work visa.

"Saleema, you will not be entering the United States today," Mario said. "Please wait over there until they escort you out of the airport." He pointed towards a special exit where another officer was standing with his arms crossed.

I was in shock. I couldn't imagine starting over in Canada, after growing roots in Washington, D.C., for nearly five years.

I called my family to pick me up. I cried all evening until my younger cousin performed energy healing on me, and eventually I was emboldened to try a new tactic.

The next day, I went back to the airport to try to re-enter the U.S. as a tourist. I got Mario again. He looked at me with his eyebrows raised and said, "So, what's the story today?"

"I'd like to enter as a tourist while I sort out my paperwork."

"I'll let you in for two weeks."

"Aren't I allowed to go for 180 days at a time?"

"I'm giving you two weeks. Take it or leave it."

I would have two weeks to find a job to get myself a work visa. This lifequake thing was not letting up. Just a year before, everything seemed easy. I had landed a dream job in international development, often traveling to Latin America to work with governments, while still running side hustles, offering pro bono consulting, and having fun salsa dancing and scuba diving. I had already founded and sold two companies. I owned my own home and a rental property. At only twenty-seven years old, I had checked all the boxes of what I thought success meant.

No problem, I told myself. I'd gone through worse challenges and come out fine. But it didn't feel fine. My lifequake had messed with my mojo big time. And now my strategy to recover was off to a rocky start.

Starting With Self-Ideation

"The journey of a thousand miles begins with a single step."

- Lao Tzu

I needed to find new work fast. When I got to D.C., I took a deeper look at who I was, what I was great at, what I loved doing, what I cared about, and what I had accomplished. I turned these questions into a **Self-Ideation** tool.

I started by reflecting on my "What." Who was I? Who did I want to become? Okay, not sure there. I skipped ahead to the other three quadrants and started to draw up my "Why" Statement: a one-liner of my life's purpose. But I wanted so many things. I loved innovation and entrepreneurship. I was passionate about international development. I enjoyed marketing. I couldn't commit to one "Why" Statement! Gah!

SELF-IDEATION

SKILLS

What do people say I'm great at?

PASSIONS

What would I do if I knew I couldn't fail?

VALUES

What do I most care about?

EXPERIENCE

What are my greatest accomplishments?

ADAPTED FROM IKIGAI BY AKIHIRO HASEGAWA.

I needed to get out of my own head. Time was running out. All the introspection wasn't helping, just as it hadn't helped in India.

Desperation made me become proactive. I opened my contacts list and reached out to everyone I knew, asking if they'd be willing to meet for coffee. Friends, colleagues, former classmates, ex-boyfriends, ex-bosses. Everyone I could think of. I scheduled eight to ten coffees a day in cafes around the city. I had to change from coffee to caffeine-free tea so I could sleep. I still couldn't access my burned-out home, so when I wasn't in a meeting, I hung out in my car, did deep breathing, prayed, and prepared for meetings—all the while trying hard to remain positive.

This was the birth of **The 100 Coffee Challenge,** a process I later used to research much of this book. At the time, though, I didn't think of it as a tool. I just needed to find work that came with a visa.

People were more willing to help than I had imagined. Some of them made powerful introductions, while others connected me to valuable communities. I ended up being mentored in many meetings. In others, especially with entrepreneurs, I played the mentor role, reminding myself of my own skills and passions. With every coffee, I could feel myself transforming as I nurtured existing relationships and built new ones. It was disorienting, because I wasn't finding myself—*they* were finding me.

THE JOHARI WINDOW

<table>
<tr><th></th><th>KNOWN TO SELF</th><th>NOT KNOWN TO SELF</th></tr>
<tr><th>KNOWN TO OTHERS</th><td>
OPEN
What I and others know about me.
Keep practicing my self-awareness skills.</td><td>
BLIND
What I don't know about me, but others know about me
Get more feedback from others.</td></tr>
<tr><th>NOT KNOWN TO OTHERS</th><td>
HIDDEN
What I know about me, but others don't know about me
Share more about who I am.</td><td>
UNKNOWN
What neither I nor others know about me
Engage in active introspection</td></tr>
</table>

ADAPTED FROM THE JOHARI WINDOW BY PSYCHOLOGISTS JOSEPH LUFT AND HARRY INGHAM.

My therapist had shown me **The Johari Window** tool shortly before my lifequake, to help me balance the known with the unknown and see where I needed to find new ways of approaching myself. It came in handy now.

I had spent most of my life pleased at being HIDDEN—I knew myself fine, and others didn't know me well. These coffees helped show me I had it backwards. I was more BLIND than anything—others saw me far more clearly than I saw myself. What I thought I was great at was very different from what others thought I was great at.

I understood that to "find myself" I had to go outside, not inside. I had to let go of who "I" was, and embrace who "I" would become, and realize that this search was about following leads, more like a detective story than meditation.

By about coffee number fifty, I became comfortable being vulnerable, and began to open up about how terrified I actually was of what would happen if I couldn't find work.

A colleague named Dorte Verner empathized. An economist and award-winning photographer[3], she was fascinated by the unique way I had applied my business and marketing experience to my work in international development. She was working at the World Bank on the refugee crisis in the Middle East and Africa, and offered me a short-term project to conduct research on different types of climate-smart technologies.[4]

I was saved! But not quite. She couldn't promise more than a couple of months of work. Not enough to get me a long-term visa. I was going to have to keep drinking coffee.

Relationships Are Mirrors

Our outer world is merely a reflection of our inner world. Our interactions with others are a reflection of how we're showing up.

"How do you know what you think when you haven't heard what you've said?"

- Shamini Dhana, Social Entrepreneur

Ever heard yourself say something and think, "Did I just say that?"

I think I know myself, but in truth I'm caught in my implicit biases, early childhood conditioning, cultural nuances, dogmas, beliefs, and so on. I often don't know what I think until I say it. My real thoughts often stay hidden in the subconscious, undiscovered until I deep dive or someone draws it out of me.

As I connected with more and more people for coffee, I realized something important: prior to my lifequake, I didn't practice self-love. I didn't make time for myself. Worse, I drowned myself in people who weren't aligned with my values. I actually attracted those people because I never identified my values. I kept trying to fix everyone and everything to avoid dealing with myself.

I had been in a relationship with one man (let's call him Pierre) in which I felt connected on a level I had never experienced. I felt like I had met the male version of myself. I became obsessed with understanding more about this synergy. Pierre felt the same way.

Pierre was holding up a mirror. When he said, "I don't really want a relationship right now," it was me talking through his voice.

I kept complaining about Pierre running away from me, when I was the one running away from myself. My relationship with Pierre helped me find unconditional love and wholeness within myself. I realized that I wanted love and commitment, but was scared to express it. In fact, I usually expressed the opposite and held myself back from healing from past relationships.

When I changed my relationship with myself, it was incredible to experience the immediate transformation of my relationships with others. I started attracting people and opportunities aligned with my values and who I was becoming.

"We don't see the world as it is, we see it as we are."

- Anais Nin

Embracing Active Introspection

Innovation is an accelerated journey of personal transformation.

Whenever I try hard to innovate, I fail. Why?

After having led or contributed to hundreds of Design Thinking[5] and innovation workshops around the world, from North America to Europe to Africa, I have realized that the importance of self-awareness is highly underrated in the innovation space. I'd been trained to focus on developing empathy as the first step in the innovation process, but how can we truly empathize with others if we don't first understand ourselves?

Through the coffee conversations, I was forced to start to practice what I now call **Active Introspection** to help me discover who I was and give me cues on who I was about to become.

Active Introspection = Self-Ideation + Feedback + Action + Vulnerable Sharing

ACTIVE INTROSPECTION

PRACTICE SELF-IDEATION

Reflect on my skills, passions, values, and experience.

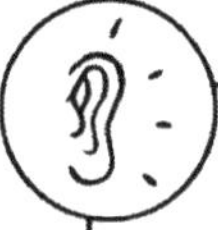

GET FEEDBACK

Share conversations with people I know, people I don't know, and people outside of my industry.

TAKE ACTION

Act on the feedback I receive by further exploring my strengths.

SHARE VULNERABLY

Lean in to my discomfort and share who I am as I continue conversing with others.

By practicing Active Introspection to develop self-awareness, I got better at knowing my strengths and weaknesses, and understanding the differences between myself and others. While it felt safe interacting with like-minded people, interacting with those very different from me, especially from outside my industry, accelerated my growth and led to more opportunities.

Rohit Bhargava, futurist and trend curator, talks about how we have become narrow-minded and open-minded at the same time. It has never been easier to access information, yet many of us live in bubbles, where we attract and interact with people who are similar to us.[6]

Gregg Brown, author and change agent, says, "We are each an apprentice to change, not its master, which means we must stay open, learn, and adapt." With continuous learning, we develop more curiosity, strengthen our self-awareness, and avoid obsolescence.

When I was unhappy in my first job, I used to stay up late Googling problems to solve. This never helped solve the main problem—myself. During the lifequake, I wasn't THINKING about innovating, I was DOING it. I was taking necessary actions in order to survive. Each challenge forced me to come up with new ideas. Each failure led me to new "Aha" moments.

Michael Lee, an innovation strategist and the editor of this book, maintains that self-innovation happens naturally if we let it. "The biggest innovation you will ever make is to innovate yourself," he says. "And yet, it's also the easiest if you just stop working so hard to have your identity block it."

It makes sense. I get creative thoughts when I'm taking a shower or a walk. Yes, great ideas and solutions can come from white-boarding, Post-its, and group brainstorms. But I best enable my own innovation by unlearning what has been programmed.

Most revolutionary innovations and business ideas don't manifest in a controlled environment. They happen by accident, when people are facing constraints or finding themselves in survival mode. Control often impedes innovation, by dampening the natural spark that sets off the fire.

Steve Jobs went to India in search of enlightenment as a teenager. It gave me great pleasure to know he too went on such a search. Marc Benioff, CEO of Salesforce, mentioned, "If you look back at the history of Steve and that early trip to India. . .he had this incredible realization that his intuition was his greatest gift. His message was to look inside yourself and realize yourself."[7]

I heard a story from a former Apple employee who had picked thousands of strawberries in order to buy an Apple II computer in the early 1980's. Over a virtual coffee, he told me:

"Steve's wisdom is from being an orphan. He wasn't trying to be a technologist. He scared people into staying late at work so they could turn his ideas into great products that he would never have been able to invent himself. Steve was aware that he was a visionary and needed others to execute."

Steve Jobs was fired from Apple before he came back to lead the company. I was also fired from a company I had co-founded right before my own lifequake, so I resonated with Jobs' story, and have come to realize that there is a correlation between personal growth and business growth.

When I examine my failures and successes, I see that my biggest breakthroughs didn't happen in an innovation workshop. In fact, as a Design Thinking expert, I realize the process itself often hinders innovation. There is one major component missing from both the Design Thinking process and the innovation space as a whole: SELF-AWARENESS.

I'm not saying one has to go through trauma to innovate. My point is that it takes a certain amount of self-awareness and resilience. It takes a personal transformation journey, since the future of innovation is about how human one can remain in this age of automation.

Innovation starts from the inside out. It starts with understanding who I am, what I do, and what I want. When I come to know myself, it's easier to define where I'm headed and how I can make an impact.

Strengthening Awareness Of Self-Awareness

"95 percent of people believe they are self-aware, but the real number is 12 to 15 percent. That means, on a good day, about 80 percent of people are lying about themselves—to themselves."

- Dr. Tasha Eurich, Organizational Psychologist

Dr. Eurich's research shows that self-awareness is the foundation for high performance, smart choices, and lasting relationships. Her work made me see that there are different types and varying levels of self-awareness. The **4 Self-Awareness Archetypes** tool below lays it out.

THE 4 SELF-AWARENESS ARCHETYPES

	HIGH EXTERNAL SELF-AWARENESS	LOW EXTERNAL SELF-AWARENESS
HIGH INTERNAL SELF-AWARENESS	 **SELF-AWARE** + I know who I am and what I want to accomplish − I seek out and value others' perspectives = I fully realize the true benefits of self-awareness ☆ Continue practicing self-awareness	 **SELF-ABSORBED INTROSPECTOR** + I am clear on who I am and what I stand for − I don't explore my blind spots or ask for feedback = This harms my relationships and limits my success ☆ Seek feedback more often.
LOW INTERNAL SELF-AWARENESS	 **PEOPLE PLEASER** + I tend to be likeable and integrate well in teams − I feel depleted from putting others' needs before my own = I overlook my values and make choices that don't serve me ☆ Introspect more often	 **PURPOSE SEEKER** − I don't yet know who I am or what I stand for − I don't know how others actually see me = I feel frustrated with my performance and relationships ☆ Share my authentic self more often

ADAPTED FROM THE FOUR SELF-AWARENESS ARCHETYPES
BY TASHA EURICH, ORGANIZATIONAL PSYCHOLOGIST, RESEARCHER, AND AUTHOR.

I was a serious **People Pleaser** for many years, and thought I had to morph into what others wanted me to become. I thought that developing self-awareness meant doing lots of self-reflection, and I ended up with lots of blind spots. I spent too much time in my head and turned into a **Self-Absorbed Introspector** during my Eat, Pray, Self-love trip. As I went through the 100 Coffee Challenge and shared more about myself, I became a **Purpose Seeker**, aiming to develop awareness as to who I was going to become.

Arianna Huffington, Founder and CEO of Thrive Global and Co-Founder of The Huffington Post, spoke with me in depth about the importance of taking microsteps to develop self-awareness. Huffington defines **microsteps** as small, science-backed steps we can start taking immediately to build healthy habits that significantly improve our lives. She shared her three favorite microsteps that we should proactively apply.

1. **"Create a transition to sleep, which starts by disconnecting from the news and social media, which are really frankly full of stressors. We need that time to disconnect and unwind before we can surrender to sleep and fully recharge."**
2. **"Our breath is our superpower. Most of us breathe unconsciously, but it takes sixty seconds to course correct from stress. Stress is unavoidable—you're never going to have a stress-free life, but cumulative stress is avoidable. Any time you feel stressed or between Zoom [meetings], take 60 seconds to focus on your breathing. Navy Seals use box breathing in times of stress: Inhale to the count of 4, pause to the count of 4, exhale to the count of 4. If you have trouble sleeping at night or get stressed during the day, you can practice box breathing."**
3. **"Remembering at different times, when you're washing your hands or washing the dishes, three things you're grateful for. It doesn't have to be big things. I'm grateful**

about my cup of coffee in my favorite pink cup. It's a joy trigger. When you remember what you're grateful for, it starts different neural pathways in your brain. Gratitude is truly the greatest antidote to stress."

Ripples, Not Onions: Emptying Our Cups

"You never arrive. It's always a constant rediscovery. It's very personal how people do it. I do it by taking a step back and using tools. What I use in business I use in my private life."

- Alexander Osterwalder, Creator of the Business Model Canvas

A year before the lifequake, a close friend had said to me, "You don't spend much time alone. I wonder if you're scared of what you'll find, and so you distract yourself by keeping busy."

And then shortly after that, Pierre too told me that I wasn't introspective enough and suggested that I seek professional help.

Nonsense. I spent plenty of time on my own! Hmm. Then I realized that even when I was alone, I was always doing something to distract me from being with myself.

My therapist told me, "We'll peel back your layers to get to your core, like an onion."

I learned a great deal in those therapy sessions, but, each time I thought I was "done," something would happen that would trigger the need for more work. I never got to the core of the onion. And I realized this old metaphor of being an onion does not work. I feel more like a RIPPLE: constantly moving, having an impact. An onion sits still. A ripple never does.

"In the minds of geniuses we find, once more, our own neglected thoughts."

- Ralph Waldo Emerson

According to Emerson, the difference between the creative and the uncreative mind isn't that the creative person has different thoughts. They both have similar thoughts. It's just that the creative mind takes them seriously, while the uncreative one discards them. Great ideas don't always feel like brilliant insights. They often feel like trivial thoughts accompanied by a lot of doubt. The fear of coming off as boring or weird continues to quash an enormous number of good ideas. The ability to bring forth an idea requires a certain level of confidence, which comes from self-acceptance.

Working on myself starts by accepting that I'm perfectly imperfect. In fact, I've started telling people that I'm a recovering perfectionist.

An older gentleman, Tony, who was a professional meditator and executive coach, added me on LinkedIn. For some reason, when I met him for coffee, I felt drawn to Tony, as if he was an oracle. I blurted out everything I was going through. Then Tony said two words that changed my life.

"Stop searching."

These words hit me like a rock in the face. Here I thought that all the searching I was doing was the whole point. Suddenly, I felt that the progress I was making was an illusion. What did he even mean? Was he telling me to focus on "being," and not getting stuck in "analysis paralysis?" That overthinking everything was leading me to self-sabotage and keeping me running on a hamster wheel? Was he trying to calm down the anxiety I was trying so hard to hide? Two simple words, and yet they shook me to my core.

Tony's comment reminded me of a story I had once heard about a Zen master, Nan-in. Once, Nan-in received a university professor who came to inquire about Zen.

"Open my mind to enlightenment," the professor said.

Nan-in smiled and said they should discuss the matter over tea. He began to pour his visitor a cup. He poured and poured and the tea rose over the rim and began to spill onto the table and splash onto the robes of the professor, who finally shouted: "You are spilling the tea all over me! Can't you see the cup is full?"

Nan-in stopped pouring and smiled at his guest. "You are like this teacup, so full that nothing more can be added. Come back to me when the cup is empty. Come back to me with an empty mind."

Remembering that story, I understood what Tony meant. My teacup needed to be emptied. New ideas need time and space to grow. I was trying to reinvent myself while still stuck in my old beliefs. The more Tony listened to me, the more I started hearing myself. It helped me pour out some of my current thinking so I could make room for Saleema 2.0.

As my work with the project in Haiti was about to end, I grabbed coffee to catch up with Dorte. It turned out that she had received funding to continue the work we had started with the temporary food security project. By reaching a state of relaxed awareness—allowing a stream of consciousness to come through my mind and body—I became a magnet for opportunities that were aligned with my new state of being.

The gig also gave me a visa for another year so I could continue my reinvention journey in the place I needed to be. What had been my main aim now felt more like a bonus—my new self-awareness was the real prize.

Key Takeaways:

Starting With Self-Ideation
To strengthen self-awareness, I practiced self-ideation by reflecting on what I'm great at (skills), what I love doing (passions), what I care about (values), and what I have accomplished (experience).

Relationships Are Mirrors
I learned most about myself through those around me.

Embracing Active Introspection
When I was feeling stuck and wanted to be proactive in reinventing myself, I went out and talked to a hundred people. I had meaningful conversations with people I knew, people I didn't know, and, especially, people from outside of my industry.

Strengthening Awareness Of Self-Awareness
The extent to which I do my inner work and cultivate self-awareness is the extent to which I'm able to show up as an innovator.

Ripples, Not Onions: Emptying Our Cups
By creating space and emptying my cup, I attracted opportunities aligned with who I was becoming.

"INNOVATION IS ABOUT BEING HONEST WITH YOURSELF. YOU HAVE TO BE HONEST IN ORDER TO INNOVATE."

- ALEX FERNANDEZ-GARITA
CORPORATE SOCIAL RESPONSIBILITY LEADER, JOHNSON & JOHNSON

"WHEN WE GET OUT OF THE BUSYNESS, AND CARVE OUT TIME TO LET OUR MIND RELAX, IT BECOMES EASIER TO DISRUPT AND **INNOVATE** OURSELVES."

- TOM LAPLANTE
CHIEF STRATEGY OFFICER, INSPIRE.WORLD

"*Be aware of the filter* YOU'RE HEARING PEOPLE THROUGH."
— ASHLEY PALLATHRA, THERAPIST + AUTHOR

"**INNOVATION** STARTS WITH I BECAUSE YOU HAVE TO UNDERSTAND WHO YOU ARE, WHAT'S YOUR **PURPOSE**, WHAT ARE YOUR **STRENGTHS**, AND APPLY THAT TO YOUR STARTUP."

- CRISTINA COLLAZOS
STARTUP INVESTMENT PROGRAM MANAGER
CITY OF KNOWLEDGE

"YOU NEED TO HAVE BREATHING ROOM TO TAP INTO **CREATIVITY** AND **INNOVATION**, WHICH IS SPACE TO THINK AND DO THINGS DIFFERENTLY."
- DIYA KHANNA, DIVERSITY + INCLUSION LEADER, AMAZON

"**GROWING YOUR OWN SPIRITUAL GARDEN,** A HAVEN FOR AN EXHAUSTED OR CYNICAL MIND, IS THE ONLY WAY TO STAY ON THE PATH OF DOING SOCIAL AND ENVIRONMENTAL OR CREATIVE WORK WITH REAL, MEASURABLE IMPACT WITHOUT CAVING IN TO DESPAIR."
- LEILA JANAH, AUTHOR + SOCIAL ENTREPRENEUR

"~~**DISRUPTION**~~ USED TO BE FOR THE PRIVILEGED FEW, NOW IT'S GOING TO BE A SKILLSET THAT EVERYONE WILL NEED TO EMBRACE."
- REUBEN ABOOTORABI, FOUNDER + CEO, THE AUSTIN AGENCY

"WE ALL HAVE A BANK OF INTERNAL **WISDOM** AVAILABLE TO US. WE DON'T HAVE TO THINK ABOUT IT A LOT. WE NEED TO BE FREE FOR IT TO SURFACE."

- JIM WILLIAMS
GLOBAL LEARNING ADVISOR

WE OFTEN CHECK THE ASSUMPTIONS OF OUR BUSINESS CASES BUT NOT WHAT WE'RE ASSUMING ABOUT EACH OTHER AND HOW THE WAYS WE **INTERACT** AFFECT US AND OUR OUTCOMES.
- ELENI PALLAS, EXECUTIVE COACH + ORGANIZATIONAL ACTIVIST

ADVERSITY IS
AN OPPORTUNITY
TO REINVENT OURSELVES

Chapter 2

Insightful Curiosity

Priming My Creative Mind

The fish were dead. All of them. Hundreds in the room-sized tank. I stood next to Dorte at the Museum of Natural History in Palestine, just outside Bethlehem, both of us silent as we tried to unravel this catastrophe.

I had been really excited to visit this aquaponics farm to validate all the research we had been doing. Aquaponics seemed like the perfect circular economy solution to address food insecurity in developing countries—the plants feed on the fish poop, and the fish feed on the plants or the algae that grows on the plants.

But now, on the ground, I realized that aquaponics might not be as easy as we had assumed. The museum manager explained that they had experienced a power outage, causing the aquaponics system to fail and the fish to die. Over the next couple of weeks, it just got worse, as every aquaponics farm we visited exhibited failure after failure.

This put us in a tough position. Senior leadership hadn't believed this innovative idea of ours would work, yet we had kept fighting for it. Now it looked as if they had been right all along. And we couldn't think of another solution that would provide both produce (fruits and vegetables) and protein (fish) symbiotically. We still had more site visits to make, so there was some hope left, but at this point we were pretty sure our research would never pay off the way we had hoped.

From Curiosity To Insights

Don't kill your ideas. Archive them while you go through learning cycles and iterations.

I thought back to a year earlier when this all started. I was sitting in an office in Washington, D.C. conducting research, and everything seemed possible. This was my first project working on food insecurity, or anything to do with agriculture. I also had zero experience working with refugees. There I was, a non-expert, trying to come up with a solution for refugees half a world away, in countries I had never visited.

It turned out that my inexperience was very useful. Working in something totally foreign forced me out of my comfort zone. I was glued to my computer, reading hundreds of articles and journals on everything from hydroponics, aquaponics, and aeroponics, to vertical farming and 3D printing.

I brought Dorte to a food tech event in New York City where we met the award-winning restaurateur and chef José Andrés, the Founder of World Central Kitchen, and the leading serial entrepreneur Gary Vaynerchuk, more popularly known as Gary

Vee. We sampled hydroponic vegetables, 3D-printed pizza, toasted crickets, and kale ice cubes, tried out an innovation lounge with interactive sound and food-tasting experiences, and learned about some of the most advanced food system innovations in the world. We even participated in a taste test for different types of insect bolognese sauces.

None of the solutions seemed appropriate for the refugees' circumstances because they didn't hit **The Innovation Trifecta.** They weren't human-centered.

The Innovation Trifecta by IDEO, a global design and innovation company, represents the ideal innovation process, meaning that a solution is viable, feasible, and desirable.

Viable: Would these high-tech solutions have a sustainable business model and could they be scaled?

Feasible: Would these solutions work both technologically and operationally?

Desirable: Would the refugees even want these solutions?

THE INNOVATION TRIFECTA

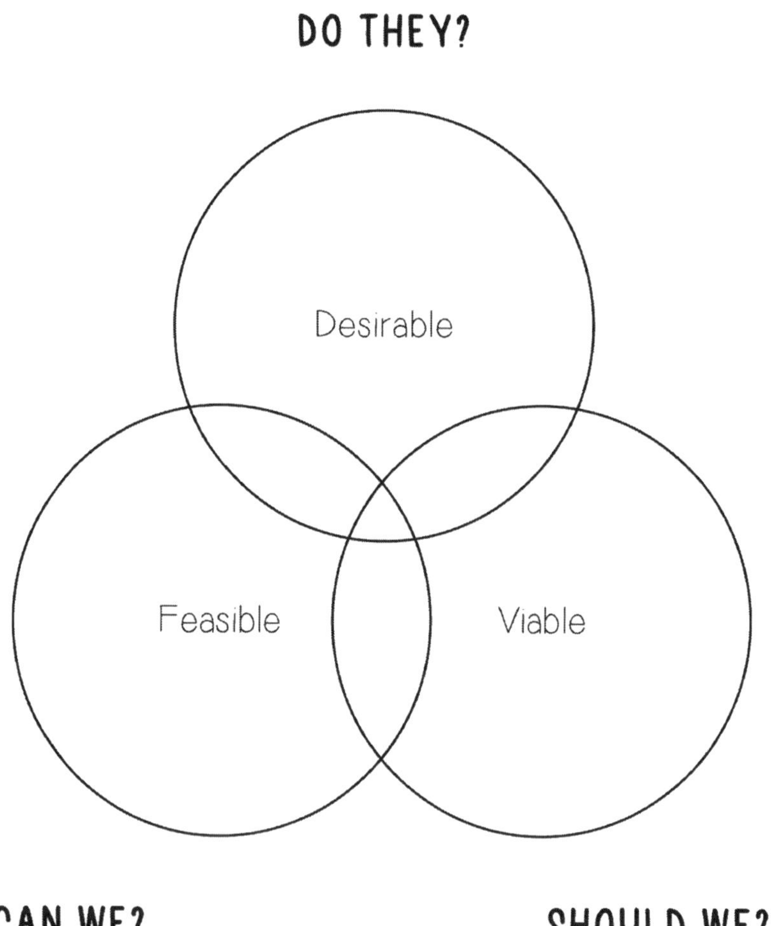

ADAPTED FROM THE THREE LENSES OF INNOVATION BY IDEO

I hadn't visited the refugees to see if they would be willing and able to adopt these methods—I had been limited to reading the research published online. All the methods seemed far too complex, and no one had yet done what we were looking into, combatting the food insecurity of the refugee crisis with innovations in soilless farming.

We decided to hit the pause button while we sought funding to continue our research. We knew a breakthrough would eventually come, but it required us to gain a better understanding of the problem we were trying to solve.

Benjamin Atkinson, Innovation Engineer at Toyota, says it's important to archive ideas and not kill them. He says that we don't know how many learning cycles we have to go through, which may involve archiving our current project because of limitations on timing, technology, or expertise.

Becoming Comfortable With Being Uncomfortable

We need to move out of comfort to move into growth.

Several months later, Dorte shared some great news: we had received a grant to expand the research.

We embarked on a search for less sophisticated yet still climate-smart solutions. But I had exhausted all the literature I could find on innovative food systems. I was terrified that the whole project would be a failure.

FROM COMFORT ZONE TO GROWTH ZONE

GROWTH ZONE

HERE'S WHERE YOUR EPIC IMPACT HAPPENS.

LEARNING ZONE

WHAT EMPOWERED ACTIONS WILL YOU TAKE?

FEAR ZONE

WHAT LIMITING BELIEFS DO YOU HAVE?

COMFORT ZONE

DON'T STAY HERE TOO LONG.

Fear of failure is often what stops us from being creative. Growth happens when we're uncomfortable, but most people prefer to spend time engaged with activities that make them comfortable. Being aware of what discomfort feels like and leaning into our edge a little more than we usually would—even in microsteps, like Arianna Huffington suggested—can help us become comfortable with discomfort.

As you can see in the **From Comfort Zone To Growth Zone** tool, we have four different zones: Comfort, Fear, Learning, and Growth.

Our **Comfort Zone** is what feels safe to us: for example, our daily routine. Going to work every day, paying bills, picking out clothes to wear in the morning, and so on. Don't stay here too long.

Our **Fear Zone** is where our limiting beliefs live, the ones that hold us back from our hidden talents and untapped potential. It's this fear that leads to our best ideas remaining in the closet.

Our **Learning Zone** can be slightly uncomfortable, though we're curious and motivated to learn. This is where our empowered actions happen, often reframed from our limiting beliefs, enabling growth and impact to take place.

Our **Growth Zone** is where we track our progress on our impact metrics and where we can maximize our impact. It's where the ripple impact happens.

You can identify your **limiting beliefs** for each idea in the Fear Zone, come up with **empowered actions** to help you get to your desired impact in the Learning Zone, and list your **impact metrics** under the Growth Zone.

Limiting Beliefs: The untrue stories you tell yourself that hold you back from making your maximum impact.

Empowered Actions: The activities you'll pursue—even in micro-steps—to overcome your limiting beliefs.

Impact Metrics: The indicators you set up to measure the progress of your empowered actions towards the impact you strive to make.

The goal is to maximize the time in our Learning and Growth Zones and become aware of the triggers we feel when we're entering our Fear Zone. Hence, the importance of taking baby steps when trying something new.

What's keeping you in your Comfort Zone? Is it your job, your career path, or your relationship?

Reframing Rejection: From Furious To Curious

Adversity is an opportunity to reinvent ourselves.

I was in our hotel in Israel when I got the call. Our trip to Gaza to visit an aquaponics project was being canceled due to lack of a security clearance.

Only a few days before, I had almost not flown to Israel, because while I was on the way to the airport in Washington, D.C., Dorte called to tell me that senior leadership had canceled a major part of our trip, to Lebanon. We decided to press forward with what was left anyway. And now, this.

Thankfully, I had started a 100 Coffee Challenge dedicated to this trip, and had come across an article about a nonprofit project training asylum seekers to grow produce on an apartment building rooftop in Tel Aviv. I contacted the founder, Lavi Kushelevich, who connected me to nearly every industry expert across Israel.

Soon we were traveling around the country, even making a couple of trips to Palestine to see what turned out to be the dead fish. We visited a commercial hydroponics farm in Jerusalem that delivered fresh produce boxes to locals. We met two entrepreneurs outside of Ramallah who were building a commercial aquaponics farm to sell produce to restaurants.

But it was at our last site visit in the Palestinian Territories where the light bulb turned on. We were at a research institute that was piloting similar work to what we were trying to do, although they didn't have refugees in mind. They were addressing food insecurity among Palestinian women while generating income opportunities for them to sell the surplus produce. They had put together simple hydroponics systems using recycled and upcycled materials: pipes, buckets, solar panels. We hadn't come across such simple systems before. The rejections had led us to a major breakthrough.

We were excited to present the successful case study to senior leadership and prove that our idea was possible. But our leadership was still resistant. Nevertheless, I stayed resolute about the power of asking. Even if it seems like we're asking the impossible, the worst that can happen is we get rejected. And then we move on. It's human to fear rejection. But asking and being rejected is critical to progress, similar to the notion of testing and failing forward.

Caring about what other people think is a major block to developing a creative mindset. Some of the most accomplished leaders with wild, crazy ideas were considered eccentric. The greatest ideas and innovations are often rejected at first, but their inventors keep grinding away and eventually win.

Thomas Edison's teachers told him he was "too stupid to learn anything," and he was fired from his first two jobs. It took him ten thousand microsteps to invent the lightbulb. He even said,

"I didn't fail ten thousand times. The light bulb was an invention with ten thousand steps."

The truth is that other people's doubts trigger my own doubts about myself. It's human nature to be self-conscious, but there is often a fine line between using intuition before making a decision, and judging myself based on my limiting beliefs.

Jia Jiang is an entrepreneur who helps people overcome their fear of rejection, build resilience, and turn rejection into opportunities. When I learned of his methods, I became fascinated by his work. He put himself through what he calls Rejection Therapy, with the goal of getting rejected every day for a hundred days in a row to desensitize himself to the pain of rejection.

As an advocate of experiential learning, I felt inspired to introduce a similar exercise to students in my Design Thinking and entrepreneurship classes and leadership workshops, called the Rejection Ritual, especially since resilience is an important trait for entrepreneurs and leaders—well, to be honest, for humans in general.

I incorporate the "get out of the building" approach from Lean Startup methodology, where founders of startups go out and talk to customers to test their hypotheses. I ask my students to roam surrounding streets in pairs with the objective of getting rejected as many times as possible. They can ask strangers for anything, the more unlikely the better: a ride across the country, citizenship from a foreign embassy, or a hug (before COVID-19!).

It encourages them to think outside of the box and come up with wild ideas that are more easily rejected. They shoot videos, and we watch them and laugh together. The exercise helps them reframe rejection as fun and empowering while they practice curiosity and build resilience.

Reversing Our Assumptions

The dots don't always connect in the way you are used to.

Sand blew into my eyes through the windows of the SUV. I could barely see, which was probably best as we bumped over the divots in the dirt—I couldn't call it a road—grabbing the dashboard, the head cushion of the seat in front of me, that little hook above the window you're supposed to hang things on, anything to stay in my seat. This kind of drive was normal in Djibouti, a small, water-scarce country in the horn of Africa. It was scorchingly hot, fifty degrees Celsius, more than 120 degrees Fahrenheit.

My team and I had just visited the Ali Addeh refugee camp, which hosts nearly 20,000 refugees from Eritrea, Ethiopia, and Somalia. We were now on our way to a town called Obock to visit the Markazi refugee camp, which hosts over 2,000 refugees from Yemen. Many of these refugees face food insecurity, nutrition deficiencies, water shortages, little access to electricity, harsh land and climate conditions, and unemployment.

After seeing the value of going beyond Google and learning about the hydroponics systems in the Palestinian Territories, I now wanted to get a better understanding of the problem we were trying to solve. I wanted to experience what was happening in the refugee camps and hear from the refugees firsthand.

We started this new cycle by challenging and reversing our assumptions. Assumptions are the worst roadblocks of all. Invisible, insidious, and habitual, assumptions stop us before we even start. Take a look at the image below. What's the first thing you'd do?

CONNECT THE DOTS

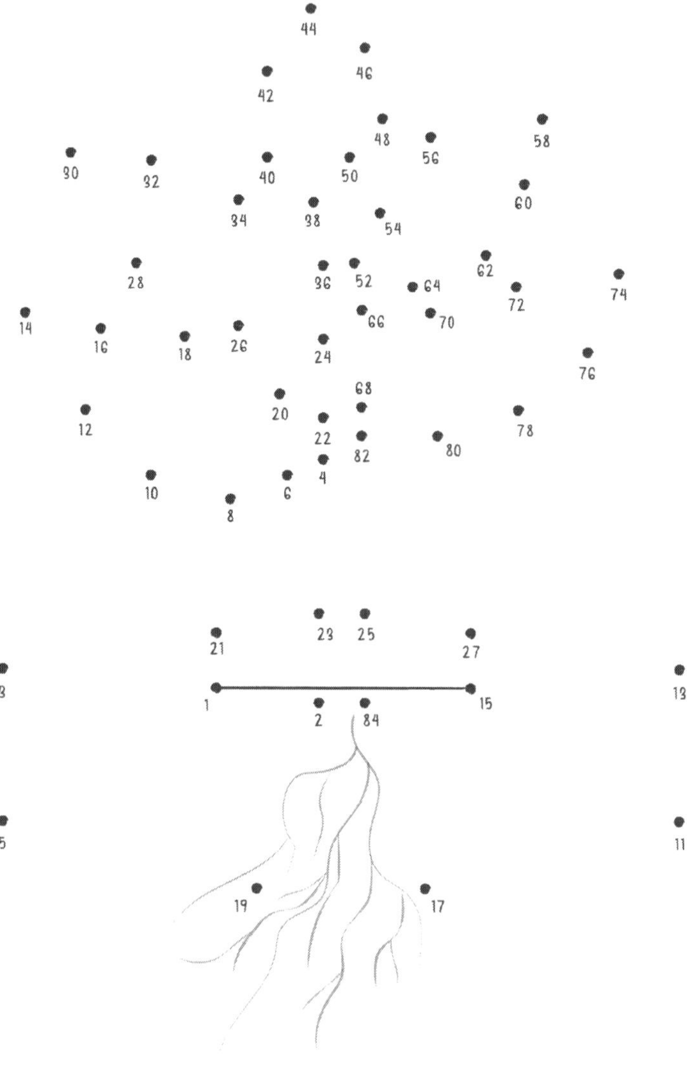

Connect all the odd numbers from 1 to 27 and then connect the even numbers from 2 to 84.

If you think drawing a line from 1 to 2, and from 2 to 3, seems like the most logical thing to do, you're right—but wrong. You've made the obvious assumption. You learned this way of doing such a puzzle from those "connect the dots" exercises from childhood. But this puzzle is different. In this puzzle, you need to connect all the even numbers and then all the odd numbers. What do you see when you try that? That's right, it's a hydroponics plant!

Try showing this exercise to someone and see if they make the same assumption about going in numerical order. Most people do.

It's human nature to make assumptions. It saves us time and energy. Even the best innovators do it. According to *Freakonomics*, Thomas Watson, the founder of IBM, said in 1943, "I think there is a world market for about five computers."[8] That was thirty years after he started the company, known for being a pioneer in business computing.

It's important to be aware of our assumptions so we can challenge them. What assumptions are you currently making in your life and work? What would happen if you challenged them?

When we rolled up our sleeves in our research process, expanded our team, and visited projects in other countries, we were able to reverse our assumptions, as shown in the Reversing Our Assumptions tool. We realized that the simplified hydroponics systems could actually be adopted by the refugees—and met The Innovation Trifecta after all.

REVERSING OUR ASSUMPTIONS

Can hydroponics address food insecurity amongst refugees?

EXISTING ASSUMPTION	REVERSED ASSUMPTION	NEW SOLUTION IDEA
The refugees don't have access to the resources needed for hydroponics.	The refugees can use their existing resources to make hydroponics work.	We can leverage local and recycled materials to create simplified, adapted hydroponics systems.
Hydroponics isn't profitable and requires significant startup capital.	Hydroponics can be executed with low costs and can increase economic opportunities.	We can pilot low-cost systems building off of previous successful experiences in water-scarce regions.
Senior leadership won't support our idea because it is unprecedented and has a high risk of failure.	Senior leadership considers our idea innovative and will support us.	We can educate senior leadership about the benefits of hydroponics.
A = B	B = A	A = C

Context Switching Using Curiosity

"When you come out of a startup-founding experience, you get to a place where you get broken and remade as a person. It's a whole new level of exposure to ambiguity, chaos, and risk."

- Anand Dass, Director at Facebook and Investor

Anand Dass is a former entrepreneur who is now a technology leader at Facebook. He talked to me about the process of going from entrepreneurship to intrapreneurship. He calls it context switching.

"Some people go from one startup to the next startup to the next startup. After exiting my own startup, I asked myself: Where do I find a problem space that I'm familiar with that I can work around again? I didn't want to have to start from scratch."

Dass found an opportunity at Facebook, which operates like a startup. Sometimes we need to move away from the startup context to rebuild emotional resilience while learning and growing into the next version of ourselves.

I have to give lots of credit to Dorte, who gave me the reins to manage our project. She valued my creativity and let me do things my way when we got stuck. She let me create a vision for how I saw the project being successful as if I were an entrepreneur-in-residence. She didn't discount my ideas, as unrealistic as they often seemed.

I had now gone from an experienced entrepreneur to a novice **intrapreneur**—an employee tasked with developing an innovative idea or project within an organization. I could contribute to making a huge impact with all the resources needed and with a team. I could learn a lot without taking on all the entrepreneurial risk. After my lifequake, this was a relief.

I applied the 100 Coffee Challenge again to gain insights into solving the food insecurity problem. Going into the field, to the refugee camps, in countries across the Middle East and Africa to better understand the situation of the refugees made all the difference.

In the Markazi refugee camp in Djibouti, the Yemeni refugee community came together to welcome us and discuss their challenges collectively. It turned out that they had agricultural backgrounds from home and in many ways knew far more than we did.

Being on the ground, I learned about many solutions that were not in our database. I discovered techniques to grow food that use zero soil and up to ninety percent less water than traditional agriculture. Many of these techniques, especially the simplified ones, were not covered in our literature reviews. They were not, in other words, Googleable.

Just as "you are what you eat," you are the information you take in. You're unlikely to come up with creative solutions to problems by staring harder at the problem.[9] Instead, you should learn from experiences that challenge your worldview.

Innovation doesn't come from simply reading material that everyone has access to. Reading can help inspire you, but the light bulb switches on when you get out of the office and talk to people on the ground who face the challenge you're addressing.

"Innovation doesn't only happen in the lab. It happens on the street every day."

- Mary Tafuri, Vice President of Global Sales at IBM

Associative Thinking: The Power Of The Marginal

"We shouldn't be afraid if we're not an expert. In fact, we should take on jobs in areas where we're not an expert so that we nurture our curiosity and learn to master new skills. Knowledge is the only thing that grows when shared!"

- Mary Tafuri

I've never been able to keep a single plant alive, not even air plants. Sometimes I wondered why Dorte chose me to help lead this project. But that was the exact reason she chose to bring me on board. She liked that I was an outsider with an ability to think outside the box.

Not being an industry expert was challenging, but it also forced me to speed up and learn what wasn't being examined by those "in the know." Having a creative space to discover possibilities enabled me to think that anything was possible.

When trying to innovate, we shouldn't keep looking in the same place we've looked already. We have to shift elsewhere and look for insights that are invisible as of now. One way of seeing the invisible is by asking outsiders, people who don't carry the same beliefs.

Sometimes the most innovative solutions are simple and already exist in some form. Neither refugees nor hydroponics are new phenomena. Hydroponics has been around for centuries. Food insecurity amongst refugees is common. But no one had connected these dots.

Associative thinking is the ability to connect unconnected ideas. It's one of the key skills that distinguishes innovative leaders. It's often referred to as **cognitive flexibility**, the ability to restructure knowledge to adapt it to different contexts.[10]

According to the World Economic Forum's "Future of Jobs" report, innovation, complex problem-solving, ideation, and flexibility are in the top ten skill groups that will set professionals apart in the future of work.[11]

Cognitive flexibility is at play when a consultant is switching among clients in different sectors, or when a serial entrepreneur moves among startups. For example, after our research on hydroponics to address food insecurity, we noticed another problem. Hydroponics was helpful in water-scarce areas, but it didn't produce enough volume of crops to feed the population, and lacked sufficient protein.

We expanded our research to look into insect farming. Insects are an extremely efficient source of protein. We learned that combining insect farming with simplified hydroponics would contribute to the circular economy and help vulnerable populations increase their economic opportunities by selling the surplus produce and insects.

The best way to strengthen cognitive flexibility starts with asking good questions. As a former terrible question-asker, who was often told as a child to think before opening my mouth, I've had to come a long way to understand how to ask better questions.

BAD QUESTIONS VS. GOOD QUESTIONS

DO YOU THINK THIS IS A GOOD IDEA? Only the market can dictate this.	**WHAT INSPIRES YOU TO DO WHAT YOU DO?** Helps get to the real problem.
HOW MUCH WOULD YOU PAY FOR X? Unlikely to be a valid, qualified answer.	**WHAT ARE THE IMPLICATIONS OF USING THIS SOLUTION?** Helps distinguish between real problems and annoying problems.
WOULD YOU USE X IF IT MADE YOUR LIFE EASIER? There is a bias towards saying yes here.	**TALK ME THROUGH A TIME YOU EXPERIENCED FAILURE** Stories are meant to "show, not tell."

TIPS

TALK LESS AND LISTEN MORE.

LEARN ABOUT YOUR CUSTOMER'S LIFE INSTEAD OF FOCUSING ON YOUR IDEA.

ASK QUESTIONS THAT INVITE A STORY.

Great Minds Think Unalike

Diversity is a catalyst for innovation.

"And the award goes to. . ."

I couldn't believe it. We won an award from the World Bank for our research study.[12] We were at a cocktail reception shaking hands and taking photos. We had received so much resistance to our project initially, it seemed impossible that we would come this far and have our work create an impact on the ground in developing countries.

Before our project, no one had addressed the problem of refugee hunger using hydroponics. We "created" this combination. Now it has become an area in which many startups and organizations are working. Millions of people are adopting this approach each year. The World Food Programme recently launched the H2Grow program at their Innovation Accelerator to implement hydroponics in Chad, Sudan, Zambia, the Palestinian Territories, Namibia, Algeria, Kenya, Jordan, Peru, and many other countries.[13] Some developing countries have moved on to use hydroponics for community and commercial production outside of using it to help refugees.

It had now been two years since my lifequake. Back then, all I wanted was to surround myself with like-minded people, who could relate to my scary experience.

But now I had become comfortable with being uncomfortable. I knew we weren't going to get anywhere if I stayed within a homogeneous group of experts. We needed the right recipe for an innovative team with diverse personalities and skill sets.

I needed to learn from people on the ground and listen to real stories of those I was trying to serve. Looking inside the organization wasn't going to help. It was best to keep a distance while my team and I did our research.

The award didn't mark the end of our research. It served as validation to keep going, and was a catalyst to scale up our work to make a bigger impact. As the years have gone by, aquaponics has been working for some populations, so our initial assumption has been proven wrong. And the success of our first study led to the need for another: how can we mix hydroponics with insect farming to address food insecurity?

The world's food production systems, including traditional agriculture and livestock production practices, are unsustainable for the planet. Neither the consumption of insects nor hydroponic crops is new; humans have been eating both for many years. However, farming insects and hydroponic crops to achieve development goals is a new and innovative development approach, especially for vulnerable communities, such as refugees or others who live in extreme climates that do not support conventional farming.[14]

That's a story we're still working on.

Key Takeaways:

From Curiosity To Insights
Never throw away or get rid of ideas—keep them aside until the timing makes sense, the technology exists, and the right talent is in place.

Becoming Comfortable With Being Uncomfortable
Learning and growth happen when I move out of my comfort and panic zones.

Reframing Rejection: From Furious To Curious
My most challenging times are my greatest opportunities to innovate.

Reversing Our Assumptions
When I reverse my assumptions, I can think about ideas, opportunities, and solutions in ways I haven't thought of before.

Context Switching Using Curiosity
I practice curiosity by applying existing ideas to new contexts.

Associative Thinking: The Power Of The Marginal
I don't have to be an expert in order to innovate.

Great Minds Think Unalike
I shouldn't just connect with like-minded people, because innovation happens when different minds come together.

"HOW DO YOU SOLVE PROBLEMS USING DATA AS A BACKER BUT NOT AS THE SOLE PIECE? SUCCESSFUL OUTCOMES HAPPEN WHEN WE HAVE DATA BUT ALSO DIVERSE MINDS AND EXPERIENCES AT THE TABLE THAT CAN SEE A PROBLEM FROM DIFFERENT **PERSPECTIVES.**"

- ERICA YOUNG, WORKPLACE INNOVATION CATALYST, SOCIETY FOR HUMAN RESOURCE MANAGEMENT

"BE A CONTINUOUS LEARNER AND **FOLLOW** TRENDS IN AREAS THAT DON'T INTEREST YOU. YOU DON'T KNOW WHERE AN **IDEA** COULD BE HIDING."

- *Aiman Kabli*

AUTHOR + ENTREPRENEUR

"*Creative thinking* OFTEN OFFERS AN AVENUE FOR INTUITION TO GENERATE PRAGMATIC, INNOVATIVE IDEAS."

- DR. TUSHAR HAZRA

BUSINESS + TECHNOLOGY EXECUTIVE

"ORGANIZATIONS WORK LIKE BODIES. YOUR ENTIRE BODY HAS TO BE **HEALTHY** AND **CREATIVE.**"

- MONICA H. KANG, FOUNDER + CEO, INNOVATORSBOX

"WE'RE IN A MOMENT IN TIME IN WHICH YOU CAN LITERALLY **LEARN ALMOST EVERYTHING**. THE ABILITY TO LEARN IS NOT LIMITED BY WEALTH OR WIFI SIGNAL. IT'S ABOUT THE WILLINGNESS TO LEARN AND ACCESS."

- NEETAL PAREKH, SOCIAL ENTREPRENEUR + ECOSYSTEM BUILDER.

"YOU SHOULD NOT LIMIT YOURSELF TO A NARROW SET OF *ideas*. ALWAYS TRY TO DEFINE NEW AND HIGHER TARGETS FROM PREVIOUS RESULTS, ADOPTING THE **"KAIZEN"** APPROACH OF CONTINUOUS IMPROVEMENT, ENHANCING A LITTLE EACH DAY AND EXPANDING YOUR OWN PORTFOLIO OF INTERESTS AND **KNOWLEDGE.**"

- RENATO AZEVEDO SANT ANNA, DIGITAL BUSINESS STRATEGIST + INNOVATION ADVISOR

"A'S AND B'S DON'T HAVE ANYTHING TO DO WITH THE FUTURE OF WORK. THE FUTURE OF WORK IS TO BE ABLE TO **LEARN, UNLEARN, AND KEEP LEARNING.**"

- ANGIE WILEN, DIRECTOR OF STRATEGIC TRANSFORMATION, FREDDIE MAC

"WHEN LEADERS **STOP** LEARNING, THEY PUT THEIR BLINDERS ON AND THE ORGANIZATION AS A WHOLE FALTERS. IF YOU ALLOW YOURSELF TO GO STALE, YOU WON'T BE AS VALUABLE TO THE ORGANIZATION, IN YOUR PROFESSION, AND TO YOURSELF."

- **CHRIS VESTAL**, CHANGE MANAGEMENT LEADER, WASHINGTON METROPOLITAN AREA TRANSIT AUTHORITY

YOUR SWEET SPOT ISN'T
JUST DISCOVERED
IT'S DEVELOPED

Chapter 3

Intuitive Expertise

Finding My Sweet Spot

As the date of my talk got closer, I became more and more nervous. I'd never done a solo talk on a large stage, nor a presentation to innovators and leaders on innovation and leadership.

The last talk I'd done I had a co-facilitator, and even then I broke down crying an hour before going on stage. Now I was going to be doing it alone, for the first time, at a major inclusive women in tech conference in the nation's capital. In short, I was terrified and a few days before, wanted to cancel.

One of my best friends came over to my place to help.

"Your slides are nice, Saleema," she said. "But where is your story?"

"What do you mean?" I asked her, already shaking.

"It sounds like a classroom lecture. Where's the real Saleema?"

"The real Saleema?" I still didn't know who that was, much less how to share her on stage.

"Yes! The Saleema with a story of resilience. Who's been through much in her life and overcome it. Who has something to share with others at a conference like this."

To be honest, that just made me more terrified. But I took her advice and changed my whole talk, focusing on my personal story, my struggles, the lessons I had learned. It felt awkward. Before, I had always been the person behind the scenes.

I rehearsed dozens of times. I arrived at the conference with my slides printed out, even though the conference manager had assured me that I'd be able to see the presenter's view of my slides on a screen in front of the stage. While I was waiting to go on stage, I scribbled out dozens of notes on the print-outs. Teeny tiny text. But it wasn't tiny enough to fit. Whatever confidence I had left was gone.

When I got on stage, a miracle didn't happen. No presenter's view, and I realized my notes were so small and cramped that to read them I would have to stand there staring at the stack of papers, which would be a disaster for the audience. I couldn't even figure out how to use the slide clicker. I looked out at the hundreds of people looking back at me, laughed nervously, and went totally blank. Then I folded up my notes, ditched the podium, and started to talk.

Finding My Sweet Spot: What, Not Why

"Finding our sweet spot starts with the inward journey. Understanding what makes you get up each morning. What's the value for other people there? Who am I? Who do I want to be?"

- Eva-Marie Muller-Stuler, Chief Data Scientist, IBM

I had started up another 100 Coffee Challenge. I kept having to leave the country every ninety days to renew my visa, and I was fed up. I needed more permanent work. But subconsciously, I was aiming at more. I didn't realize it then, but later I understood I was trying to figure out: Who am I going to become? And more importantly (I thought): WHY?

In all these conversations, I started to notice a pattern.

"You're all over the place." "You need to specialize in one thing." "What exactly do you do again?" "I'd love to help you but I'm really not sure how."

In short, I needed to figure out who I was. I could see their point. I was teaching an entrepreneurship class to graduate students, facilitating leadership and innovation workshops, doing a bit of public speaking, had started coaching, and was helping other coaches market themselves. I would be confused, too, if I were having coffee with myself. I looked more deeply at my skills and experience:

WHO AM I?

I'm a problem solver.

I connect people.

I'm a certified coach.

I advise entrepreneurs and business leaders.

I love seeing growth and change.

I amplify people and organizations.

I have a background in economics and monitoring and evaluation.

I teach entrepreneurship and design thinking.

I provide consulting to international organizations.

I teach business owners how to hire and manage remote teams.

I have conducted research on food security and hydroponics.

I worked in Haiti on post-earthquake urban reconstruction.

I've lived in the Dominican Republic, Brazil, and Italy and traveled to 70+ countries.

My regional expertise includes Latin America, the Middle East, and Africa.

I have run a couple of digital marketing agencies.

I speak five languages fluently.

Well, that wasn't any less confusing. And this list could go on.

No wonder people couldn't figure me out. I didn't know how to describe what I was about, so they didn't either. I started asking people how they perceived me as a description rather than a specialty.

"Dynamic hustler." "Broad talents." "All over the place." "A master generalist." "Jack of all trades, master of. . .some?" "A mess."

I approached my mentors for advice. They too told me that I should put all my efforts towards specializing in a specific sector, since that's what helped them succeed.

"What's that one thing you could be known for that you can do really well?" They asked me. "What's your sweet spot?"

I tried to do what my mentors said. But I couldn't. I wasn't interested in a nine-to-five job that would define me. I had studied economics, but I didn't want to be an economist. I was passionate about international development, but I didn't want to become a bureaucrat.

Looking inward gave me no clear answers—each day my inner voice said something different. Looking outward wasn't the solution—each conversation just left me more confused. It took a toll on my confidence. I even subscribed to a mindfulness app. That didn't help either: I just fell asleep most of the time.

The fact was, I enjoyed wearing different hats and being in different spaces. And I was good at it! I had, after all, worked twenty different jobs in the last twenty years! I often didn't know what I'd be doing six months ahead of time, or even what country I'd be in. Almost all my gigs had come through networking, not resumes. I changed my LinkedIn profile every time I was trying to get a new gig.

I was a specialist at being a generalist. And what was so wrong with that?

Generalists are able to adapt easily to fast-changing circumstances and can innovate by leveraging and combining their different skills in unique ways, especially to solve the complex, uncertain problems we're already facing in the future of work.

David Epstein, the author of *Range: How Generalists Triumph in a Specialized World*, emphasizes that the way to succeed is by sampling widely, developing a breadth of experiences, embracing detours, constantly experimenting, while juggling various interests. His research shows that future top performers do not pick and stick. They try a variety of instruments, sports, and activities in an unstructured or lightly structured environment, gaining a multitude of different skills.

"But nobody solves a problem by hiring a generalist," some people still insisted. They had never heard the term "polymath" and thought it had something to do with algebra.

Okay. If I had to specialize in something, I thought, here it was: I want to reduce the failure rate of entrepreneurship. I want to help more entrepreneurs succeed. But that wasn't a job, a position, or a role with a title. I had no idea how I could make it possible in reality.

I eventually realized the problem was that, in trying to specialize, I was seeking a purpose to the specialization—a reason WHY. Simon Sinek, author of *Start With Why*, famously insists that WHY is the most important question to ask. I have come to disagree.

You may, funnily enough, ask, why?

So let me tell you. "Why" is an important question to ask in certain situations. But it turns out it's a very wrong question to ask when it comes to self-awareness and intuition. We simply do not have access to many of our unconscious thoughts, feelings, and motives, which leads us to invent answers that may feel true but are often inaccurate representations. We end up believing our bias and living in an illusion.

Let me show you what I mean. Between A and B, which do you think is longer?

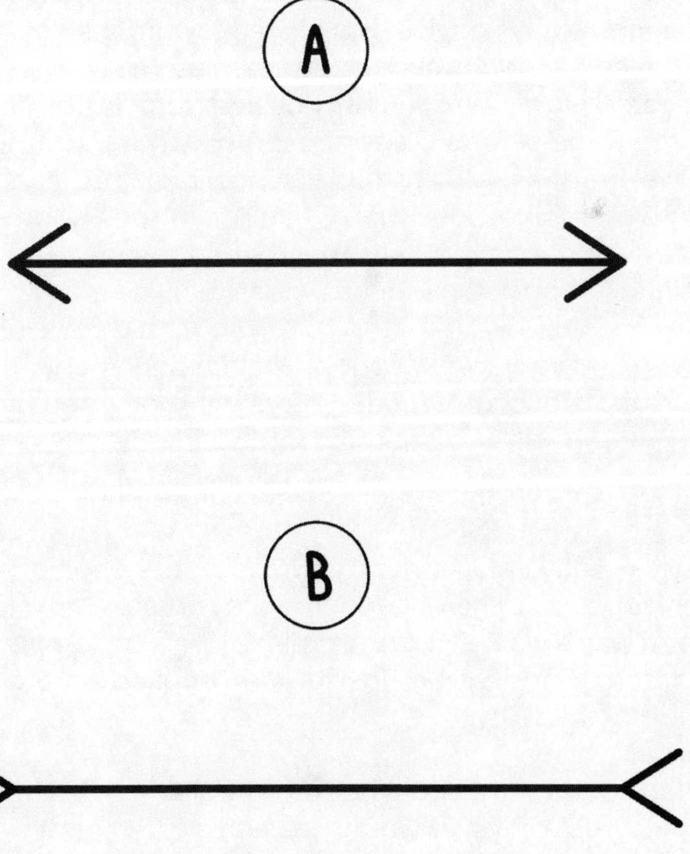

For most people, B is obviously longer. But it's not. They are the same length, but the arrows at the end make B look longer. This example shows **cognitive bias** at its best.

Cognitive bias is a strong, preconceived notion of someone or something—a mental shortcut our brain produces to expedite information processing—based on information we have, perceive we have, or lack.[15] This simple illusion demonstrates how we can be tricked by irrelevant information. The arrows aren't part of the line, and we know that, yet it just looks longer. We can't get rid of our biases, but when we become aware of them, it can help.

I consulted coaches to help me find my "Why," and discovered that each coach's advice was biased toward their own expertise. The career coach suggested job roles. The business coach suggested plowing through my business goals. The life coach told me to adjust my career based on what I want from my life. The therapist said I should first heal past traumas. I ended up with more questions than when I'd started. By focusing on the "Why," I became a Self-Absorbed Introspector, limited to revisiting my past experiences. I felt stuck.

> "You find your sweet spot by first finding your intrinsic motivation. Most innovators are motivated by something intrinsic."
>
> - Jeremy Agnew, Social Entrepreneur

I finally asked a close friend of mine at the peak of her own career for advice. She whiteboarded my career chronologically. It took a whole weekend. We examined all my accomplishments in each role and, at her insistence, focused on the "What" instead of the "Why."

Shifting to the "What" provided a great breakthrough. I had spent a couple of years waking up with a different "Why" statement every day, based on my emotion or influence from others and not by facts and evidence, skills and experience. By examining everything I had done, it was much easier to find the throughline—the "What" that later would become my "Why."

Inspired to make the Johari Window more actionable, innovative, and future-oriented, I adapted it into the **Sweet Spot Mapping** tool to help me find my sweet spot.

SWEET SPOT MAPPING

EXCELLED AT

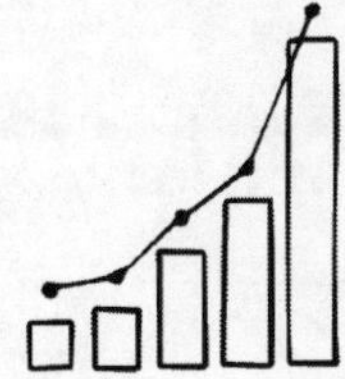

PRAISED FOR

LOVED DOING

OPEN TO TESTING

You can do the same for yourself. Take a flipchart, whiteboard, or piece of paper, and map out all the projects you've either led or contributed to in some way, whether personally or professionally. Don't think too hard.

EXCELLED AT
What projects did I excel at the most? I'm confident in these skills and others know I have them too.

PRAISED FOR
What projects garnered positive feedback? The praise I received from others may have surprised me.

LOVED DOING
What projects gave me the most joy? Think about the projects I'm so passionate about, I'd do them for free.

OPEN TO TESTING
What projects have I been keeping on the back burner? What projects out of my comfort zone am I willing to try out?

Intuitive Ideation

Our sweet spot is not just discovered, it's developed.

"You can have multiple sweet spots—they are intertwined. It's all about owning your story, where you are at that point of your life and career, and being okay with it. You fall down, you pick yourself up, you brush off, you keep going."

- Cate Luzio, Founder and CEO of Luminary

The Open To Testing quadrant is hardest to fill in. It is a space to discover and develop untapped potential.

Have I thought of starting a blog or podcast? Have I been wanting to write a book or do more public speaking? The ideas and projects I'm open to testing are often where innovation lies.

The process of filling out the Open to Testing quadrant requires **Intuitive Ideation**—tapping into my unconscious mind to bring out the ideas I already have. What are some of the ideas that pop up when I silence my thoughts and amplify my true inner voice?

When ideas don't easily come to mind, I have learned to ask friends and colleagues what types of projects or activities they think I should pursue based on what they know about me. I sometimes share the three filled-out quadrants to give them context.

I used to think that once I found my sweet spot, work would feel like perpetual bliss, that I wouldn't even feel like I'm working at all. It doesn't work like that. My sweet spot doesn't always come naturally. Sometimes it takes effort.

Thomas Edison famously said, "Genius is 1 percent inspiration and 99 percent perspiration."

Being great at what I'm most effective at requires me to step out of my comfort zone. Many professional speakers still get nervous before going up on a big stage, but the love they derive from seeing the results outweighs their discomfort.

"Follow your passion" is one of the worst pieces of advice on the planet. I often tell my students not to chase their dream job. Instead, they should find a job or gig that will challenge them and take them out of their comfort zone, and get paid to learn things that will train them to implement their vision and build the foundation for their business.

Incorporating passion into my life's work is important, but what I have done to sustain myself has not always been the most meaningful. My goal has always been to move away as fast as possible from trading my time for money, which gives me more time to focus on my passion on the side if necessary. Seeking profit for my passion has paid off sometimes. Other times it's been a recipe for exhaustion and burnout.

Add Value First, Sort It Out Later

"As we grow, our sweet spot shifts. The process of finding our sweet spot starts with framing. Most people think about the context of work, rather than framing their work as a journey of self-discovery. We should be on a journey where we're constantly clarifying and refining our values. What are things we're good at vis-a-vis other human beings?"

- Hariraj Vijayakumar, Founder and CEO of Designs In Change

I ended up spending a lot of time trying to "find my passion" and figure out my optimal career path. Every time, this left me feeling more stuck than when I started.

Then I realized that to find my sweet spot, I had to add value to others first. Being honest with myself was the first step. I joined a couple of nonprofit boards, helped organize a conference, ran events for local entrepreneurs, and did volunteer work. I learned a lot about my sweet spot in that process.

Daniel Kahneman, psychologist, economist, and author of *Thinking, Fast and Slow*, says we shouldn't trust our intuition; we should test it.[16] He defines intuition as, "thinking that you know without knowing why you do." He considers confidence as a very poor cue to accuracy, "because intuitions come to your mind with considerable confidence and there is no guarantee they're right." Kahneman says the following three conditions need to be met in order to trust one's intuition:

1. **Regularity in the world. "Chess players have it. Married people have it. People who pick stocks in the stock market do not have it."**
2. **A lot of practice.**
3. **Immediate feedback. "You have to know almost immediately whether you got it right or got it wrong."**

After getting direction on my sweet spot, I had to test and iterate, as with any innovation. I had to take action first and only then spend time sorting the results and repositioning myself.

> "Intuition is a trainable faculty. Don't just follow your intuition, which is very context- and time-specific. Educate, train, and verify your intuition."
>
> - Rohit Sharma, Product Design Engineer

I was born with my instincts, but I've acquired my intuitions over my lifetime. I have no intuitions independent of a specific domain. My intuition is similar to a powerful computer system, but because it's unconscious, it's error-prone.

Sharma suggests becoming mindful by listening to the body and measuring the accuracy of intuitions on a scale from one to ten. Improving my intuition in this way has helped me prioritize and make better decisions.

Hybridpreneurship: Paving My Unique Path

We're not defined by what we do, but who we are.

"We often find our sweet spot through experimentation. It usually happens in bite-sized pieces over long periods of time. It's more of a continuous-learning, building-block type of thing, instead of simply rolling the dice."

- Neil Kleinberg, Tech Entrepreneur and Adjunct Professor

"No employer is going to want to hire an entrepreneur. They can't sit still in a job."

This was the worst piece of advice I was ever given. It was from a career counselor while I was in graduate school. She recommended I remove the word "co-founder" from my resume and suggested I use "freelance writer" and "translator." I listened to her, ignoring my gut feeling, because I was still young and inexperienced and didn't know yet that I could pave my own path.

Thanks to this sage input, I spent years pursuing work that didn't feel aligned with who I am. But at least doing what I didn't like doing helped me realize what I do like doing. I learned to leverage my experience instead of beating myself up over it.

In fact, overcoming this bad advice helped me shape my sweet spot. All these years later I was able to ask myself a simple but essential question: Why did I have to choose between being an intrapreneur and an entrepreneur? Why couldn't I be both? Wasn't there a way to leverage both to make a bigger impact than each of them individually?

I soon realized there was. And I called it "**HYBRIDPRENEURSHIP**."

	ENTREPRENEUR VS.	INTRAPRENEUR VS.	HYBRIDPRENEUR
MEANING	I envision and execute an innovative idea that I am passionate about while filling a need in the market	I work for an organization and use creative problem-solving skills to develop ambitious ideas into scalable solutions	I earn a living through work that enables me to pursue my passion projects while building a community
AUTONOMY	I have complete autonomy to design my own systems and processes	I have less autonomy and work with existing systems and processes	I select my level of autonomy and the extent to which I build my own systems and processes
FUNDING	I use my own resources	I use my employer's resources	I leverage resources through the different projects I pursue
RISK	I bear all of the risk of my company's failure	My employer bears all the risk of the initiative's failure	I spread risk by diversifying my income streams
BRANDING	I operate under my company's brand	I operate under my organization's brand	I am brand agnostic and establish a platform around my personal brand
REWARD	I reap the financial rewards, if my company succeeds	I earn career rewards, such as recognition, compensation, and bonuses	I reap the financial rewards and long-term benefits from building a community

We're taught to speak in the language of part-time and full-time, intrapreneur and entrepreneur. Yet innovation isn't something that's meant to label innovators and put them in boxes! Why must I decide between being an employee, intrapreneur, or entrepreneur? The multiple hats I wear while engaging in various projects ARE what make me unique.

It was time to drop all these labels, what I thought they meant, and embrace my uniqueness. To see my life as a series of projects and build a portfolio career. A hybridpreneur can be an entrepreneur, intrapreneur, or both, at various times. It's not so much about what I do, but rather, how I think, how I invest my time, and the impact I make. Being a hybridpreneur enables me to innovate in everything I do. Yes, okay, it's still a label, but a label I get to define myself.

So what makes a hybridpreneur? I define four elements: Profit, Passion, Growth, and Impact.

THE HYBRIDPRENEUR

PROFIT

Makes money to support oneself and to invest

PASSION

Dedicates time towards passion projects

GROWTH

Embraces constant learning and curiosity

IMPACT

Gives back to the community in a meaningful way

Profit: I need to take care of myself financially in order to live a healthy life. This way, I can invest in my other projects without depending on the market.

Passion: It's important to set time aside to work on my passion projects. This even includes spending time on my hobbies. Passion is the fuel of life.

Growth: I constantly need to be learning things outside of my comfort zone and be up to date on the latest trends. Embracing curiosity enables me to adapt to fast-changing circumstances.

Impact: I should prioritize giving back, whether through small, thoughtful gestures, or actively contributing my time towards an initiative I care about. Volunteering regularly can make a real impact.

Here's how I apply it:

- Consulting work (Profit)
- Helping entrepreneurs succeed (Passion)
- Teaching at a university (Growth)
- Volunteering at a nonprofit (Impact)

By engaging in various projects, my "Why" became clearer as I made twists, turns, and pivots. It's just like starting a business—I may have an idea, but the actual problem I'm solving may not be clear until I get started and go through learning cycles and iterations and eventually pivot.

In fact, it is starting a business. The business of ME. After I started seeing my career as a portfolio, and myself as my business, I found myself creating jobs and opportunities out of what seemed like tiny projects. For years I was ambivalent about running a business, until I realized that I AM my business.

How Do I Know If I'm A Hybridpreneur?

Life doesn't have to be about climbing an upward ladder of jobs. It can be a series of projects.

"We need to get out of black and whiteness. Job descriptions are dated. We should practice job crafting, and allow individuals to embrace what gets them out of bed every morning and the value they bring to the organization."

- Angie Wilen, Change Management Leader at Freddie Mac

The best way to future-proof myself, I realized, is to create a portfolio career as a hybridpreneur in order to diversify my skill set, build multiple income streams, take on passion projects, grow, and leverage the community I build. It's become easier to grow a personal brand by embracing my unique gifts.

Diversifying hedges me against the uncertainty of the future. It also keeps me engaged, relevant, and in different spaces that add value to others. I don't need to compartmentalize myself, but rather be flexible in the different projects I engage in.

Becoming a hybridpreneur may not resonate with those who are drawn to pursuing and staying in highly specialized careers, though anyone can embrace the concept. Not everyone wants to be a hybridpreneur. How do I know that I am one?

SIGNS OF A HYBRIDPRENEUR IN THE MAKING

I'M HUNGRY

I have a lot of drive. I could spend every waking minute on my mission, which is a major part of my life's work. I want to better productize myself.

I'M AN IDEALIST

I have a strong passion to make an impact on our world. I dream big, even though I may not have the structure and direction to realize my vision.

I LOVE COMMUNITY

I don't want to be on this path alone. Building a support network is important for accountability and my success.

I LEAN TOWARDS AN UNCONVENTIONAL PATH

I don't want to settle for less than what makes my heart sing. I love new challenges, wearing multiple hats, and changing up what I do.

MY DEFINITION OF SUCCESS OFTEN SHIFTS

What I thought I once wanted isn't really what I want right now. I've had to redefine what success means to me more than once.

Finding My Sweet Spot By Stopping The Search

My sweet spot has a simple name: MINE.

Oh yes, and that talk at the conference that started this chapter—how did it work out?

I froze for a moment in front of those hundreds of people, with too-small scribbled notes and no cue to rely on. And then I unfroze. Not having my notes allowed me to show up as myself. I didn't say everything I had planned, and I said other things in a way I hadn't anticipated. Walking off the stage, I had no idea what people thought.

But I knew soon enough. For the rest of the day, people kept telling me how much they loved my talk, how much it inspired them, and how many practical lessons they took away from it. Several major companies and nonprofits invited me to speak to their employees. The experience left me feeling incredibly empowered, but even moreso, shocked. Sharing myself honestly had worked out great. It was one of my best talks ever.

I had found my sweet spot: SHARING MY STORY.

My story. Nobody else's. Nobody else could have my sweet spot, because it was my story, based on my life as a generalist. And most amazingly of all—a recovering perfectionist who had ad-libbed her way into the spotlight. That one experience helped me start to make peace with detaching from my script, and rewriting it a little bit differently every day.

I've become a seasoned hybridpreneur now. I provide innovation strategy consulting and workshops to organizations and business schools. I develop courses and teach graduate students and high school students, and as you'll learn more about later, I run Ripple Impact, which helps me achieve my dream of powerfully helping entrepreneurs. I still do professional speaking, and I also help other entrepreneurs share their stories.

My sweet spot, as it turns out, doesn't have a title. I can't explain it in a sentence. But I know what it is, and now you do too. And that's pretty all right.

Key Takeaways:

Finding My Sweet Spot: What, Not Why
To find my sweet spot, I started with the "What" by examining my career as a portfolio of projects in order to find the throughline—my "Why."

Intuitive Ideation
My sweet spot wasn't something I had to search deep inside for. It was something that was slightly uncomfortable—that others saw I'm great at and that I had to work at.

Add Value First, Sort It Out Later
To narrow down my sweet spot, I focused on adding value to others wherever I could, and sorting out the results later. I reflected on the things I excel at, get the most praise for, and absolutely love, while thinking about the ideas I'm open to testing.

Hybridpreneurship: paving my unique path
I didn't have to choose between being an entrepreneur or intrapreneur. As a hybridpreneur, I could embrace both—each one adds value to the other.

How Do I Know If I'm A Hybridpreneur?
I future-proofed myself by diversifying my skill set, building multiple income streams, pursuing passion projects, growing constantly, and leveraging my community.

Finding My Sweet Spot By Stopping The Search
I realized my sweet spot is unique automatically, because I am unique.

"WHEN AN ORGANIZATION BECOMES **STAGNANT OR STUCK**, ALLOWING AN OUTSIDER TO **UNDERSTAND** THE COMPANY'S STRATEGY AND OPERATIONS FROM THEIR UNIQUE **PERSPECTIVE** AND LENS OFTEN RESULTS IN VERY WORTHWHILE OBSERVATIONS, FEEDBACK AND **IDEAS**. HOWEVER, LEADERSHIP MUST BE OPEN TO HEARING THE FEEDBACK TO TRULY EMBRACE IT. PEOPLE **HAVE TO BE READY TO MAKE A CHANGE.**"

- ROBIN HIRSCH EVERHART, SVP + CHIEF HUMAN RESOURCES + TRANSFORMATION OFFICER, LOUISIANA PACIFIC BUILDING SOLUTIONS

"WE FIRST HAVE TO FIND OURSELVES AS **INDIVIDUALS**, AND BE IN FLOW, IN ORDER TO DO WHAT **WE WANT TO DO.**"

– ANDREINA MARRÓN, CO-FOUNDER + CEO, IVO TALENTS

"SOMETIMES WHAT **YOU LOVE DOING ISN'T ENOUGH.** YOU NEED TO BE ABLE TO RAPID PROTOTYPE YOUR CAREER."

- RACHEL AN

HR + INNOVATION LEADER

"WE NEED TO STAY FLUID AND NIMBLE! **WHAT IS THE IMPACT I WANT TO HAVE?** TO IMPACT **100** PEOPLE, START WITH A STARTUP. TO IMPACT MILLIONS, **CONSIDER PLAYING IN A BIGGER AND GLOBAL ENVIRONMENT.**"

–JEROME SELVA, GLOBAL MANAGING DIRECTOR, PEGASYSTEMS

IF YOUR NETWORK CONSISTS OF *like-minded thinkers*, YOU'RE NOT GOING TO GET VERY FAR. **YOU DO NEED THAT MIX.** THAT DIVERSITY, OF PEOPLE WHO ALSO HAVE **OPPOSING VIEWS** THAT CHALLENGE YOU BECAUSE THEY REPRESENT PART OF THE WORLD."

- Thos Gieskes

MANAGING DIRECTOR, OIKOCREDIT

"THE MARKET IS **CHANGING FASTER NOW.** WE NEED TO READ THE ENVIRONMENT AND SEE WHAT'S AHEAD, ESPECIALLY IN OUR MAIN DOMAIN OF EXPERTISE. **WHAT ARE COMPETITORS DOING?** BE AHEAD OF THE GAME."

- GUSTAVO ARAUJO, CHIEF OF TALENT ACQUISITION, ORGANIZATION FOR SECURITY AND CO-OPERATION IN EUROPE

INNOVATION IS REPACKAGING EXISTING IDEAS

INTO ORIGINAL COMBINATIONS

Chapter 4

Intriguing Originality

Positioning Myself Strategically

My usual Design Thinking materials were on the table: Play-Doh, pipe cleaners, Popsicle sticks, and aluminum foil. But nothing else was usual at all. I was surrounded by Liberian social entrepreneurs, at iCampus, the innovation hub in Monrovia. They were singing Happy Birthday to me, and one of them was carrying a cake out.

I had led over a hundred Design Thinking workshops at that point, but it was my first time facilitating one in Africa. They swarmed me, asking for my autograph, requesting photos, and demanding to read my book. I didn't know how to explain that I wasn't as famous as they seemed to think—and I hadn't written a book, though I'd thought about it for years now.

I was comfortable, finally, as a hybridpreneur, traveling the world and making an impact sharing my story and my knowledge. I had made it a policy for organizations that hired me to work with their employees to set up workshops like this to empower young entrepreneurs and changemakers in the local community, and it was very fulfilling for all of us. Saleema 2.0, after all.

But I realized that the minute I departed, there was nothing to leave behind except the memory of a few good hours. How could I have a bigger impact? What good was a brand new Saleema if it was all just for myself?

It was clear I needed to innovate myself to the next level, so that I could truly leverage my sweet spot. The problem was the same one that had plagued me every time I thought about writing my book: how was I going to make it original? What could I say, in a world so full of clutter, that was unique and actually worth saying?

The best ideas aren't necessarily complex, but they are far from obvious. There's a reason why the Design Thinking process emphasizes going for quantity instead of quality of ideas. I knew all this, yet I still felt stuck.

I had solved a similar problem a decade before, on my very first entrepreneurial venture, during the global financial recession, translating websites in Italy where I couldn't speak the language.

Redefining Originality: The Influenced New

Originality is not about creating new stuff.
It's about reinventing what already exists.

Okay, I mean, I had studied Italian, enough to try to get a job. I walked around Reggio Calabria for weeks with copies of my resume in a folder, figuring the brain drain of the region would help, despite the high levels of unemployment and the beginning of the Euro crash.

I got my dream job working in a restaurant kitchen—for one day, until I discovered my signature Chicken Alfredo was considered a sin, and that there is no such thing in Italy as Caesar Salad. I tried to work as an English teacher, but got rejected for not having a British accent.

My brother came to the rescue again. He suggested I use my other language skills, in Spanish, Portugese, and French, to find some freelance translation work online. I started sleeping with my laptop under my pillow, waking up again and again in the night to be the first to apply to translation projects.

I became successful as a freelance translator, then pivoted to building a team and running a remote translation agency, translating websites into multiple languages to suit the multiple .fr, .es, .it, .pt, .de domains, years before there was a gig economy and luckily a couple of years before Google Translate started automatically translating websites.

Using dial-up internet and without a credit card, experience, website, or social media, we grew into a six-figure, top-rated online translation business within six months, becoming leaders in the niche market of website translation. Soon enough, I wasn't even doing the translations, because other people were much better at it, and I realized I was really good at managing them and winning the contracts.

I hadn't planned to run a translation business. I wasn't even trying to do anything innovative. I started by trying to become a chef. It was just a lucky coincidence in which my skills (languages, customer service, creativity, writing, and communication) blended with my desperation, perseverance, and adaptability. I couldn't have planned this trajectory. I had to get started and keep pivoting.

My translation business and several subsequent ventures taught me that being DIFFERENT and DESIRABLE is what allows us to disrupt and become attractive in the market. But is this the same as being ORIGINAL?

Originality is one of the 12 Future-Proof Capabilities. But it's confusing what we mean when we say it. It needs a new definition.

Like many people, I had thought that to be original, I had to create new things from scratch. But eventually I realized that everything I do builds on something that has already been done or imagined. When I conducted field studies and analyses, I had to use existing research. I was always influenced by something else, in some way. It's important to distinguish the word **original** from similar words such as **novel** and **non-obvious**.

Novel Idea: An idea that's the first of its kind that has never been seen, used, or thought of before. A "unicorn."

Non-Obvious Idea: An idea not easily discovered, seen, or understood.

Original Idea: A non-obvious combination of existing ideas.

Earlier, I shared my experience of leveraging hydroponics (an existing solution) into food insecurity amongst refugees (an existing problem), and pointed out that the two had not been previously combined together in that way. My translation business did the same. Website translation was not a novel idea, but we made it original, combining obvious ideas in a non-obvious way. No other company in our niche had brought together freelance translators from around the world to deliver multilingual web translation services, without the use of translation software. Being freelance made us agile. Being human made us diligent. Being remote made our prices competitive.

In the Information Age, originality is more important than novelty. We don't need more new ideas. Can we even find any?

We need to leverage what we have to build non-obvious combinations of existing ideas.

> "I have no original ideas. I only have original combinations."[17]
>
> - Seth Godin, Founder of the AltMBA, Entrepreneur, and Author

Creativity is a process of mixing and matching. In trying to be novel, we may box ourselves in, and prevent creative thinking from happening.

One of my favorite books, *Steal Like An Artist*, by Austin Kleon, opened up my mind to looking at originality in a different light. After reading it, I realized that innovation is about bringing my individual uniqueness into the combinations I put together. What makes my ideas interesting is ME.

I have become open to being influenced during the process of innovation. To be clear, I am in no way advocating copying. Copying is plagiarism and theft. Influence is not. Influence is essential in the creative process. It keeps us from hitting the anxiety wall, and it is the basis of how creativity works. Influence is a push out the front door, while copying is not even bothering to get off the couch.

> "What is at issue is not the fact of 'borrowing' or 'imitating,' of being 'derivative' or being 'influenced,' but what one does with what is borrowed or imitated or derived; how deeply one assimilates it, takes it into oneself, compounds it with one's own experiences and thoughts and feelings, places it in relation to oneself, and expresses it in a new way, one's own."
>
> - Oliver Sacks, Neurologist, Historian of Science, and Author

"It's not where you take things from—it's where you take them to."

- Jean-Luc Godard

A Problem Is Not Always The Problem

"'What problem are you trying to solve?' is the most frustrating thing you can ask someone with a good idea. Not everything in the future is about solving a problem that we have today because that problem may not exist in the future. Sometimes it's just a good idea that may solve a problem you don't know you have yet."

- Mike Duke, former Chief Innovation Architect at Wells Fargo

The only problem I was trying to solve in Italy was how to eat. I wasn't trying to solve a problem for my customers. The freelance translation business success was the result of an idea, pure and simple, an idea that wasn't even my own, but one my brother had sparked.

In the worlds of innovation and entrepreneurship, there has been too much focus on trying to solve problems. When we start off with the premise that we have to come up with a solution to a specific problem, we often suffocate creativity and eliminate viable ideas by steering our thought process towards finding the perfect one. Such an approach triggers stress and tunnel vision. Often, problems have a very easy solution if viewed from a different angle. A level of stress and constraint is often good for executing time-sensitive tasks that demand focus, but being focused on solving a problem can be draining and hinder innovation.

When facilitating workshops or teaching Design Thinking, I encourage people to focus on developing ideas and refining the problem they are solving as they go along. The problem they end up addressing is often very different from the one they started with.

When I want to come up with a great idea, it's more important to first reflect on what makes me original. What's unique about my life experience? What stands out in my story? What do others admire me for?

I can now come up with problem statements for most of my past projects. But they started with ideas before they pivoted to solving a specific problem. In every case, in fact, the main problem I started with was finding a solution for myself. Innovation starts with I, again.

In Chapter 2, we discussed acting first by giving value and finding one's sweet spot afterward. The same principle applies to embracing originality first in developing ideas. Great ideas don't usually start as great ideas. Sometimes, at first, they seem terrible. A bad idea becomes a great idea through cycles of learning and iteration. That's why in Design Thinking, we focus on the quantity of ideas rather than their quality.

> "There is no such thing as a business idea that exists outside of the context of whoever thought of it. A great idea isn't truly great until it fits not just the market, but you as well."
>
> - Guy Kawasaki, Entrepreneur and Chief Evangelist at Canva

While writing this book, I got stuck trying to come up with ideas for tools for readers. How could I create something simple and impactful like the Business Model Canvas? When I let it go, ideas started flowing.

The next tool, for instance, came out of nowhere while I was having dinner with friends at a Persian restaurant in Los Angeles. My friend's husband, a scientist and patent expert, was talking about how to pitch a potential client. I got intrigued about what he said about the patent process, did some reading, and next thing I knew, I had the **Great Idea Checker.**

GREAT IDEA CHECKER

NON-OBVIOUS

How does your idea stand out?

CONCRETE

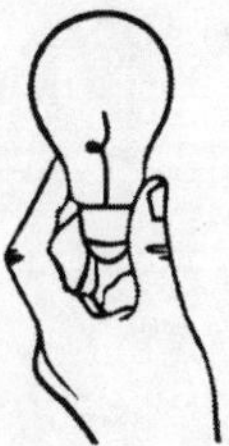

Is your idea tangible and easy to explain?

TIMELY

Why is your idea relevant right now?

USEFUL

Does your idea inspire others to take action?

I used this tool to iterate the foundation of this book, design my TEDx talk, and develop curricula. I still use it whenever I create content. My clients find it simple and valuable, something they can stick on their monitor or insert into their journal.

Is my idea non-obvious, concrete, timely, and useful?

The best business ideas evolve through learning cycles. They experience a pivot from inception to execution, and then from execution to scale. Facebook, before pivoting into a general social media platform, focused on connecting classmates from universities. Amazon, before it pivoted into an e-commerce giant, focused on selling books online.

Pagan Kennedy, the author of *Inventology*, says that ideally we would want to suffer from a frustration that is rare, that no one else knows about, and that will one day become a more widespread concern. Kennedy says that there are three types of problems: **Long-Term Problems**, **Hidden Problems**, and **Future Problems**.

3 TYPES OF PROBLEMS

FUTURE PROBLEM

It forecasts a problem that will affect thousands or millions of people in the future.

HIDDEN PROBLEM

It reveals a problem that's difficult to detect.

LONG-TERM PROBLEM

It plays out over a long period of time that inspires more and better solutions.

ADAPTED FROM PAGAN KENNEDY, AUTHOR OF INVENTOLOGY

It's important to capture the idea at an early stage, when it is raw, often before I even consider it an idea. I can get a jolt of inspiration in the middle of the night, while taking a cold shower, or going on a walk. This inspiration can also come when I am dealing with a deadline and have to quickly find a way to get something done.

In our translation business, after moving forward fast, I saw there was more demand from English to other languages than vice versa. I also realized I was better at preparing proposals, closing contracts, and retaining clients than I was at translating. So I adjusted our business to fit these realities.

The 80/20 Rule

"It's not about claiming a unique IP. It's about packaging and branding our ideas strongly in our own way. All pizzas are the same, it's the toppings that make the customer feel like they're getting a unique dish. Get to the sweet spot that clients think they're getting a highly customized solution, but eighty percent of the work and output is standardized."

- Ian Calvert, Social Entrepreneur

When I started facilitating workshops for organizations, I used to come up with a new concept for each gig, thinking that customizing each experience meant originality. That is, until one of my mentors in the industry told me that the secret is repetition with micro-improvements: at least eighty percent of the material should be standardized from past workshops with only twenty percent customized to the audience.

I asked Alex Osterwalder, creator of the Business Model Canvas, how we can continue to appear like we're doing customized work without it being customized each time, to reduce the cost and risk of failure of completely customized projects. He talked about the importance of finding the constants and variables that exist across the problems we solve:

> "Try to find problems that are very similar, consistent, and timeless across a group of people. What are the constants and what are the variables?
>
> How we run a workshop in the Middle East, in Japan, or in Switzerland is going to be very different. Yet the tool is going to be exactly the same. So what we always try to look for is the constant first—what is similar? And then we try to create that shared language.
>
> Why did the Business Model Canvas—as one tool of the many we created—work across the world, across cultures, from startups all the way to large companies? Because it's a very constant problem challenge: what's my business model?
>
> It's the same for startups, it's the same for established companies, it's the same if you're in Japan, it's the same if you're in Switzerland, it's the same if you're in the U.S. The business model is a business model, there are only a certain number of components. We don't give the answers, we ask the questions. And the questions are very constant across any culture in any context. So what we're always looking for is the constant, not the things that change."

Osterwalder agrees with the 80/20 rule: eighty percent standardized, twenty percent custom. How can you apply the 80/20 rule in your own life or business?

Differentiating Through Strategic Positioning

"The most obvious way to avoid becoming a mere clone of your competition is to truly do a better job of differentiating by actually being different."

- Rohit Bhargava, Trend Curator and Entrepreneur

In order to differentiate, Bhargava suggests looking for the non-obvious: in other words, what is different and desired yet not easily identifiable. We're living in a world where almost any idea can be copied quickly, so the only edge that lasts is based on relationships. Customers don't want products. They want experiences.

In short, position yourself strategically to attract opportunities that will pull you to where you want to be. Our translation services were differentiated from those of our competitors largely by accident. We couldn't afford expensive translation software, so we had to hire humans. Being based in the south of Italy, we couldn't find local talent, which forced us to hire online. We were able to beat our competitors' prices and speed because we were small and agile, and didn't need an office. We figured out how to work in HTML. We had strong writing and communication skills, meaning our proposals were consistently rock solid. And since we didn't actually know much about the translation industry, we didn't know what we were doing wrong.

Shortly before this book was published, a TikTok video of a method to easily prepare a quesadilla by treating the tortilla like a pie chart went viral. The idea was to put one ingredient into each quadrant, make a slit along the radius, fold the tortilla in a counter-clockwise direction, rotate it, and repeat, to form a triple-folded triangle.

Quesadillas are not a new phenomenon, but the ease, experience, and uniqueness of using this method inspired many. So I used it as the inspiration for my chart on **Strategic Positioning.**

STRATEGIC POSITIONING: HOW TO BE DIFFERENT

ORDINARY

CHEESE QUESADILLA

X Different
✓ Desired

NON-OBVIOUS

TIKTOK HACK QUESADILLA

✓ Different
✓ Desired

DESIRED

DULL

BURNT QUESADILLA

X Different
X Desired

ODD

ONION, GARLIC, AND FRUIT QUESADILLA

✓ Different
X Desired

DIFFERENT

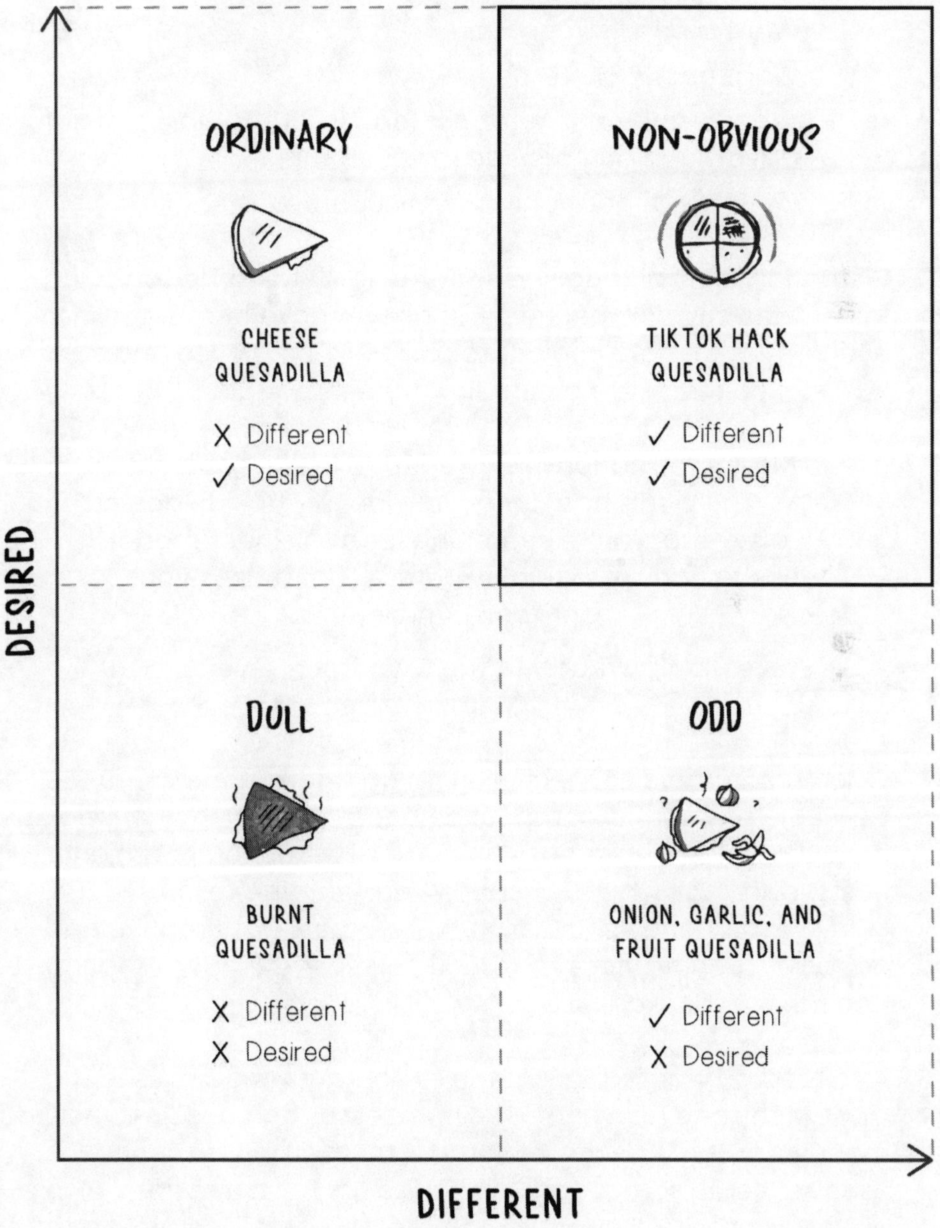

ADAPTED FROM POSITIONING: HOW TO BE DIFFERENT
BY ROHIT BHARGAVA, AUTHOR, FOUNDER, AND CHIEF TREND CURATOR OF NON-OBVIOUS COMPANY

For a business to succeed, it's essential that it focuses on both the different and desired axes of the non-obvious. Ask these questions:

- What are my strengths?
- What do my customers need?
- What's my value proposition? In other words, what advantage do I provide my customers?
- What is the positioning of my competitors?

Disruption is traditionally about being better, cheaper, and faster than my competitors. But as we move into a "feeling" economy, with more choices to pick from, employee and customer experience are becoming more important.

"Most information is shared today, unlike the old days. The world has turned completely upside down. As a startup, you're searching for a business model. It's the narrow slice of expertise that makes your company unique."

- Steve Blank, Creator of the Customer Development Method

When restaurants started opening up a few months into the COVID-19 pandemic, competition became fierce. Fewer people were going out to eat, restaurants were incurring higher costs, and many dine-in spots were earning less revenue. Many permanently shut down, while others got creative and adapted, such as those that set up extensive outdoor seating and takeout packages.

As a foodie, I wanted to visit the restaurants I had missed the most. Many had reinvented their processes and designed new menus and experiences. My most memorable experiences usually offered something unique, like eating in a heated igloo or repurposed parking lot. Many restaurants jumped on to the "design your own experience" train for takeout or offered unlimited small plates for dine-in where customers felt like they were getting a lot of value because they had more variety.

Business is all about relationships, and one thing I learned was to instill over-delivery into processes. We started offering a free sample translation in our proposal, or even a few low-cost samples for bigger projects, which made us stand out. It gave clients an opportunity to give feedback, so we didn't have to redo projects or fix them after delivering. We also incorporated more quality control by having native speakers of the target language review the translation before it got delivered. As more competitors popped up, we constantly thought of how to give more to our customers without it costing us too much.

The **Business Positioning Canvas** is my iteration of Osterwalder's Business Model Canvas, used to help entrepreneurs and hybrid-preneurs in the early stages of building a business or going through a pivot.

BUSINESS POSITIONING CANVAS

IDEA

What's your business idea and unique value proposition? Why you?

GOALS

What are your high-level business goals?

NOT YOUR SOLUTION

What do you get asked to do that you definitely don't do?

SUCCESS STORIES

What are examples of customer success stories?

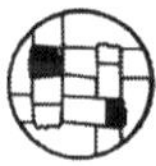

TARGET AUDIENCE

How would you describe the people who are most interested in your content, products, or services?

TEAM

What roles do your team members play? What talent is missing that you need?

DIFFERENTIATORS

What differentiates you from your competitors?

ENGAGEMENT

How do you reach and engage with your target audience?

REVENUE STREAMS

What is your current revenue? What is your projected revenue?

EXPENSES

What are your business expenses?

ADAPTED FROM THE BUSINESS MODEL CANVAS BY ALEXANDER OSTERWALDER, AUTHOR AND CO-FOUNDER OF STRATEGYZER.

Test, Test, Test

"It's always good to put yourself out there. It doesn't matter if people like your idea or not, it's really to get some feedback. So you start to understand what works, what doesn't, and then just go on and carry on but not be arrogant to say, 'hey, this is going to work' and just go—you need to constantly adapt. If you're writing a book or creating [something], it's this whole idea of having a vision, starting to test it, and adapting the path without necessarily compromising the vision."

- Alexander Osterwalder

When I started this book, I wanted to create a tool as groundbreaking as the Business Model Canvas. Along the way, Jim Williams, co-author of *Learning Paths,* advised me instead to make the whole book a transformative journey.

"All the tools exist," Williams said. "It's about putting the tools together in a new way and using them in the right sequence."

Originally I was going to call this book *Ripple Impact.* But people didn't like that title—and it later evolved into the name of my company, where it works much better. Ironically, *Innovation Starts with I* was also roundly rejected. The last thing we need, so many people told me, is another book on innovation. What does the word even mean? We suffer from innovation fatigue, to the point that its meaning has been diluted to another catchphrase.

To me, innovation is something special and different. Innovation is a human word, a timeless word, that encapsulates the creative human spirit. It is time to give innovation an expanded meaning.

Arianna Huffington said it perfectly in our conversation: "Reskilling isn't just about technical skills. It's also about the human layer on top of even the most amazing technological innovations."

Innovation starts with I. It has to. There is no place else that it can begin. That's why, to become truly innovative, I had to transform myself into Saleema 2.0, to escape my lifequake and find a new path. And now that I had achieved that, I could start to innovate beyond just myself, to what turns out to be a much more difficult step—the transition from I to WE.

We will soon see that although a personal reinvention journey feels terrific once it's completed, it's not enough on its own to make a ripple impact.

Key Takeaways:

Redefining Originality: The Influenced New
I don't need to come up with novel ideas. Instead, I can focus on creating original combinations of existing ideas.

A Problem Is Not Always The Problem
What I initially think is the problem may not actually be the real problem I end up solving.

The 80/20 Rule
I must look for the constants and variables between the problems across my audience. How can I scale up the constant?

Differentiating Through Strategic Positioning
By positioning myself strategically and incorporating my uniqueness, I can accelerate faster towards where I want to be and where I'm heading.

Test, Test, Test
When developing an idea, I should get it out of my head and test it by getting feedback from others to validate it and iterate it.

"MY WHOLE JAM IS TO LEVERAGE EXISTING MODELS TO **CREATE NEW**, OFTEN UNPREDICTABLE ONES. WHAT FURTHER DIFFERENTIATES OUR REPEATABLE AND SCALABLE BUSINESS MODEL IS THAT **WE EMPOWER CREATIVE PEOPLE TO COLLABORATE** ON THE NETWORK TO BUILD IMPACTFUL, EQUITABLE BUSINESSES THAT THRIVE."
– SHALONDA INGRAM, SOCIAL ENTREPRENEUR

WE'RE LIVING THROUGH AN ERA WHERE IT'S EASY TO BE **BOTH OPEN-MINDED AND NARROW-MINDED** AT THE SAME TIME.
– ROHIT BHARGAVA
TREND CURATOR + AUTHOR

"WHEN SOMETHING IS CONTROVERSIAL, IT ALLOWS FOR PEOPLE TO THINK, LISTEN, PONDER AND SEEK POSSIBLE SOLUTIONS."
– **ANITA NAHAL**
DIVERSITY + INCLUSION LEADER, AUTHOR + PROFESSOR

"**NATURE HAS SOLVED** A LOT OF THE CHALLENGES WE ARE GOING THROUGH. WE NEED TO BRING A MORE **BIOCENTRIC PERSPECTIVE** TO THE INNOVATION TABLE."
– LEON WANG
BIOMIMICRY PROFESSIONAL

"IF WE WERE **IDEALISTS**, EVERYONE SHOULD BE A UNICORN. **THOSE WITH STRONG BUSINESS ACUMEN COUPLED WITH TECHNICAL SKILLS** ARE LIKELY TO HAVE THE HIGHEST PROBABILITY OF SUCCESS."
ALI SHAKIL, ASSOCIATE PARTNER, IBM.

"I BUCKET PEOPLE IN THREE WAYS: **DREAMERS, DOERS, OR DRIVERS.** EACH ONE HAS A SUPERPOWER AND A BLINDSPOT. **I WANT TO DOUBLE DOWN ON THE SUPERPOWER.**"
– **SANGRAM VAJRE**
AUTHOR + CO-FOUNDER, TERMINUS

"WHILE IT'S POSSIBLE TO USE BUSINESS TOOLS WITHOUT USING THEM INNOVATIVELY, AND IT'S POSSIBLE TO INNOVATE WITHOUT USING BUSINESS TOOLS, TRULY INNOVATIVE SOCIAL ENTERPRISE WORKS AT THE INTERSECTION OF THESE TWO CONCEPTS."
– **NICOLE MOTTER**, CHIEF SOCIAL INNOVATION STRATEGIST

WE

You're now ready to move to the WE part of your reinvention journey. Even though the process of innovation starts with "I," execution happens in collaboration with others.

In this section:

- You'll collaborate and forge fruitful partnerships.
- You'll build meaningful relationships with others by communicating on a deep level.
- You'll increase your influence authentically.
- You'll reposition yourself towards your vision by telling your story.
- You'll build a foundation to scale yourself to impact the WORLD.

WARNING: You may experience some "Aha" moments that will make you rethink how you approach and build relationships going forward.

WE MIGHT START WITH WHY
BUT WE MAKE THINGS HAPPEN
WITH WHO

Chapter 5

Inclusive Collaboration

Connecting The Dots

When the COVID-19 lockdown hit, thankfully I was at home in Washington, D.C.

Yes, thankfully. For it was HOME. My visa search no longer defined my identity. I had successfully immigrated after all the struggles. And finally, I could now focus on this book. I could no longer help on the ground. Instead I could put my full energy into writing this book that everyone I served, including you, could benefit from.

It didn't go well at first. I had compiled hundreds of pages of notes on scraps of paper, notebooks, Post-its, on my cell phone, while running around the world doing workshops and other work. But I couldn't figure out how to put it together. I'd never written a book before. And this chapter was the hardest of all. How could I shift from I to WE and write about collaboration while locked up in isolation?

By luck or kismet, a couple of weeks into lockdown, a colleague of mine, Adam Smiley Poswolsky, shared in his Facebook community that he was launching an author support group. He was in the middle of writing his latest book and wanted to do it within a community. He organized Zoom sessions and I eagerly signed up.

It was a lot more fun working together. We shared stories of our frustrations and successes. We listened to guest speakers, like Adam, who'd written more books than we had. We chatted in breakout rooms. We even danced together. It had never occurred to me before that I should write a book in a group!

I found myself secretly irritated at first by the need to support so many others in the group. How would I get my book done if I was dealing with everyone else's books? And I was irritated that I was irritated—I knew myself as a generous person, who was always happy to help. Then I began to understand—I was irritated by the fact that I wasn't able to provide as much value as Adam and others, being a novice author myself.

Because of course collaboration isn't about me—it's about us. That's obvious. In today's world, we need to collaborate to be relevant and find opportunities. And even more so, to help others get opportunities. Because it's through giving to others first that we end up getting. The goal became to figure out where I could add value best.

How Can I Help?

"The more I help out, the more successful I become. But I measure success in what it has done for the people around me. That is the real accolade."

- Adam Grant, Professor at The Wharton School and Author of *Give and Take*

Above my desk I had a picture of one of the last workshops my colleague and I had done before the pandemic locked us up: the sun setting from the rooftop of The Spot, a co-working space in Marrakesh, casting a shadow over the distant older part of the city, the vast maze of the Jemaa el-Fna and the Kasbah a few kilometers away.

We were leaving for a trip through the Sahara in the morning. All the Post-its and Play-Doh in the world didn't seem like sufficient tools to leave behind for these enthusiastic entrepreneurs, just like it hadn't in the more than one hundred similar workshops we'd done in Portugal, Canada, Panama, the U.S., Liberia, and other countries.

There was a House of Beautiful Business mind map on the wall at The Spot, pictured here. I had attended the House's very first conference in Lisbon two years before, and I wondered when I saw this mural: how did this end up all the way here in Morocco?

The founder of The Spot explained that they worked in a partnership model. Of course—that's how we got me there too. A woman in Baltimore who booked me for a speaking engagement introduced me to the founder, after she had spent a month working out of The Spot during her program with Remote Year, an official partner of The Spot.

I remembered something critical about that diversity and inclusion conference I told you about in Chapter 3 and the way it came about. When I saw that the conference was coming to D.C., I intuitively reached out to the organizer. I don't know why I was drawn to it, but I knew I had to connect. I sent her a message on LinkedIn and asked her, "How can I help?"

I had no idea what kind of help she would need, but she sent me a list, and I responded to each point in detail. I made email introductions. I was genuinely interested in sharing my network to make her conference a success. I was excited to connect with people where I thought there were synergies.

I didn't expect anything in return, but she found so much value in my connecting her to people and making introductions that she recruited me as an advisory board member. She also gave me a booth, a workshop, and a TED-style talk on the main stage. I had no idea what to do with a booth and talk, but I felt it was rude to say no.

That one speaking engagement got me invitations for nearly fifty more, including being an encore speaker at INBOUND, a leading business and marketing conference, where I was asked to deliver my session twice. I also started getting paid to do keynotes just months later. It just took that one opportunity to become a platform for so much more.

Who knew that one message I had sent on LinkedIn offering some free help would lead to a ripple impact? But I should have known. Because that's how collaboration works.

In our fireside chat, Arianna Huffington said, "We need to include giving as a component of everything we're doing."

We start by taking a careful look at what would provide value to the communities we serve. What are some ideas that we're OPEN TO TESTING that could add value to our products and services? If we don't know, we do some research—ask people! We can go on a 100 Coffee Challenge to help adapt our existing products or services to make them better.

The Rise Of Unconventional Partnerships

"Competition is limiting. Cooperation encourages abundance. The survivors will be the ones who can figure out how to leverage others, integrate others, and be relevant across a wider set of others. The future of work will consist of consultants, gig workers, and boutique firms that hire each other for specific expertise."

- Coco Brown, CEO of Athena Alliance

Mark Horoszowski is the Founder and CEO of a nonprofit organization called MovingWorlds. It has a two-fold mission: getting experts to parts of the world that most need it, and ensuring a transformative experience for those who share their skills. MovingWorlds has a unique partnership model, mixing these "experteers" with corporations who want to engage their employees in volunteering and professional development, to provide skills to the organizations that need them. Horoszowski's approach to collaboration is unconventional in how it connects the dots between multiple stakeholders with such seamless ease.

Another form of unconventional partnership has arisen under the term "**Coopetition.**"[18] Coopetition is a mutually beneficial collaboration among competitors allowing them to lower costs, increase profits, and achieve higher value creation for their customers. In place of the old "winner takes all" model, coopetition provides a win/win strategy.

Coopetition has mostly been used within the tech sector, especially in collaborations between software and hardware companies that wouldn't normally compete. More and more, though, we're seeing coopetition in other industries.

Many entrepreneurs say "we have no competition." That's simply untrue. No competition sounds more like "no market." It's only in very rare cases that we are offering something totally new. Most entrepreneurs are not inventing a previously non-existent thing. Usually we're just building better mousetraps—which is more than enough.

Today isn't about the product. It's about the ecosystem. Gaining two percent of the market share each year isn't enough anymore. We need to disrupt and create new markets and win more than half of a new industry. The best way to do this is to work collaboratively.

Aside from fitting into existing ecosystems, we can also create our own. Airbnb is a great example of an invented ecosystem, a previously nonexistent digital marketplace that has created opportunities for millions of other people and businesses, including tour and transfer services, property management, cleaning services, pricing advice, and photography. Airbnb also regularly invests in and has acquired several companies that add value to their service and strengthen their internal ecosystem, such as a payments startup, a villa rental company, a city guide, a restaurant reservation app, and others.

Good ecosystems that make customers happy are hard to build, and take time. But they stand out. We need to approach unconventional partners, identify underutilized channels, and invent new business models.[19] Here's a **Stakeholder Matrix** tool that can help us think about who to collaborate with based on the level of interest and influence.

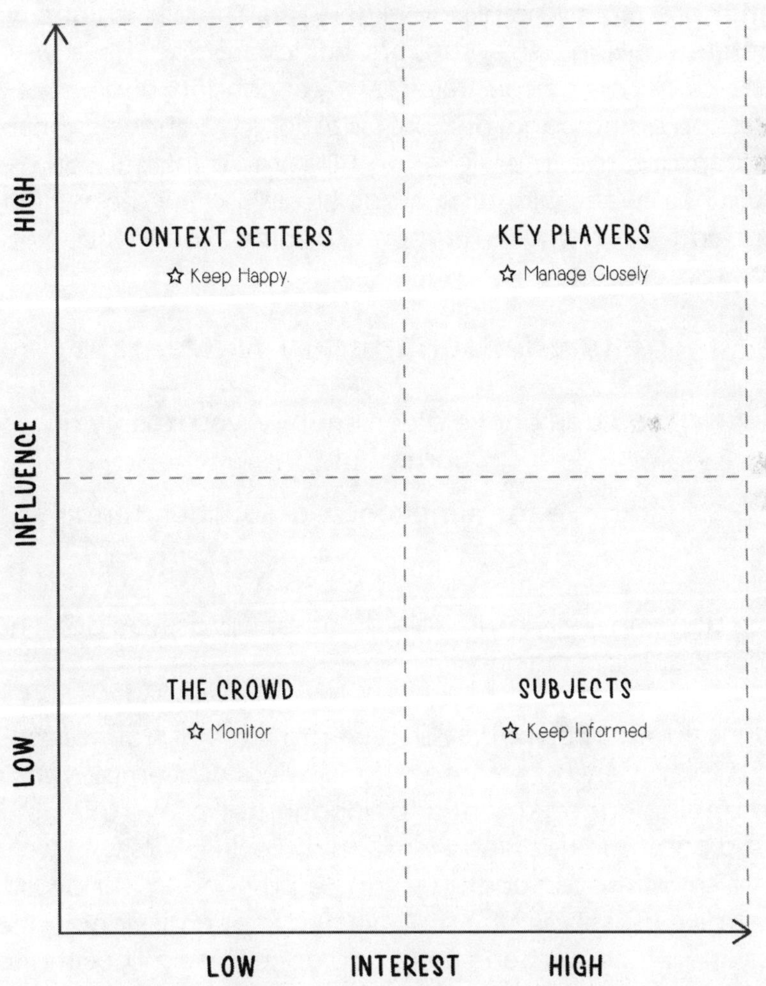

ADAPTED FROM THE STAKEHOLDER MATRIX BY JOHN JESTON AND JOHAN NELIS

Here's how this matrix applies to *Innovation Starts With I*:

Context Setters = Sponsoring organizations.
Key Players = Entrepreneurs who already know me.
The Crowd = Social media + speaking engagement audiences.
Subjects = Design Thinking workshop participants.

Using this matrix, I could see that my most powerful audience is entrepreneurs who already know me. The book alone won't reach ten million entrepreneurs. But leveraging the book correctly will get me closer, fueled by my secondary audiences—my workshop participants and organizations who have sponsored me. Perhaps the interviews and Design Thinking workshops would help when planning a book tour? I knew a transition of some sort was going to happen, but I didn't know what. Not yet.

The Niche Community Movement

"If you don't have a community, you're only a commodity."

- Sangram Vajre, Author and Co-Founder, Terminus

If you don't have a community, in other words, you don't have a brand or a business.

In our current information era, we are starving for communities in extremely niche areas. Consumers and employees are demanding engagement and accountability. We thirst to join vetted communities where we can access others who we can relate to, we have seen grow, or we have been impacted by others like ourselves who are invested in our mission and success and who have been there and done it in similar situations.

It's strategic for us hybridpreneurs to start building, as early as possible, a community around ourselves and our niche that aligns with our values and vision. This allows us to execute our work in an inclusive and collaborative way, and encourages our audience to help us accelerate by becoming part of our growth experience.

Pieter Spinder, founder of Knowmads Business School and author, maintains that as leaders, we need to build a movement around something that MATTERS—to us and to others. The movement can then become a community much more easily and powerfully.

Enrique Rubio is a great example of an innovator who has been disrupting the human resources industry by building a global community of other human resource innovators. He is the Founder of Hacking HR, a workplace innovation community and catalyst to change in human resources.

Enrique started his career as an electrical engineer and found that his skills quickly became obsolete with the fast pace of technological change. He became a leader in human resources, but after many years felt that HR wasn't really there for him. He started Hacking HR while working his full-time job before it turned into a full-fledged business. If we create better HR functions, Rubio says, we create better workplaces, and ultimately better societies.

Rubio found it hard to sustain change by himself. By collaborating, he has found it much easier to adapt to challenges. He traveled the world building chapters of innovators—HR leaders and practitioners as well as entrepreneurs, technologists, and other business leaders connected to HR. He recruited leaders in local communities to run chapters and mobilized a niche community by launching virtual summits and a Slack workspace for Hacking HR members to collaborate. This empowered Hacking HR members to become brand evangelists. He launched virtual summits featuring a wide array of voices. By practicing inclusion and enabling collaboration, Rubio grew the Hacking

HR community rapidly with over a hundred thousand engaged followers, quickly forming a global movement.

Poswolsky is another example of an excellent community leader. When he was frustrated with the lack of inclusion in the professional speaking industry, he wrote a book, *The Breakthrough Speaker*, to give aspiring speakers valuable advice that he learned as he became a professional speaker himself. He built a movement around two core ideas:

1. Professional speakers should be compensated for their work.
2. The professional speaking industry should be more inclusive.

Community members organically became ambassadors of Poswolsky's movement. And many of these ambassadors helped empower the author support group I joined. I could see that I needed to build a community to help this book make a bigger impact. And then, this book would be able to grow the community.

Building Our Solidarity Squad

We become successful by helping others become successful.

"Collaboration starts by asking the right questions. Where is there an opportunity for both businesses to win? Go deep on understanding opportunity within seemingly unconnected parts of the businesses and get creative."

- Kristy Wallace, CEO of Ellevate

At my annual catch-up lunch with a career counselor from grad school, she said, "I think you'd be the perfect fit to teach the new entrepreneurship course we're launching."

I made my way over to the career services office. The contact there was a woman I'd mentored over coffee a few years before. The application process was thorough and competitive, and I had no prior teaching experience in higher education or syllabus creation. So I just used the knowledge I had acquired and did my best.

My proposal was selected. I couldn't help but wonder how much the trust that was built with this woman years before helped me land the role. Had that one mentoring session over coffee had a ripple impact?

When we focus on giving value, it's surprising what comes back to us. We benefit by being intentional when meeting someone for the first time. Researching the person. Understanding our goals clearly. Thinking about what we need to say to get to a "yes" or a lead to the next step. Giving more, asking for less. Talking less, listening more. Making it about them. It helps to ask questions that are non-obvious and provoke curiosity, questions that might even make them smile.

QUESTIONS THAT INSPIRE COLLABORATION

UNDERSTANDING WHO THEY ARE:

What inspires you to do what you do?
What's your elevator pitch?

UNDERSTANDING THEIR LEGACY:

What do you want to be remembered for?
What is your number one goal for the year ahead?

UNDERSTANDING WHAT THEY MAY WANT HELP WITH:

If you could automate one part of your day, what would it be?
What is something you dislike doing but wish you loved?

UNDERSTANDING WHERE THEY WANT TO GO:

Who is doing the kind of work you most wish you could be doing?
What is one thing you are known for? What do you wish more people knew about you?

One of my clients, Christine, was sending out emails to get blurbs from highly influential leaders for her soon-to-be published book, and kept getting rejected. She finally asked me for feedback, to understand how she could improve.

Subject Line: Can you endorse my book, Scott? [may come across as spammy and lacks personalization]

Hi Scott,

How are you doing? I trust you're doing really well. [The ask doesn't feel authentic when it's followed by an assumption]

I included many of your insights in my book, Collapetition, which teaches people to collaborate more effectively. [Okay, good for you, but it sounds a bit vague. What's your point? Why are you contacting me? Make your request sooner if you need something from me.]

I would appreciate it if you could write an endorsement that I would include on the front cover of my book. [I'm not convinced why I should spend time on your book versus the hundreds of requests I get daily.]

I've attached my manuscript so you can take a look. [Why am I getting homework before I agree to do anything?]

Also, would you be willing to market my book on your social media when it launches? [Whoa, I don't know you. Which request do you want me to focus on? Also, why are there so many "I"s in this message?]

I'll give you lots of shoutouts when the book is launched. [I'm not asking for your help. Collaboration shouldn't always feel transactional or like tit for tat.]

Thanks a lot! [I'm not sure if you're thanking me, assuming I'll help you out, or for what exactly?]

Christine

Here is a better, more collaborative, and more authentic way to write that email:

Subject line A request from a fan, a CollabMBA alumna, and the author of Collapetition

Hi Scott,

I really enjoyed your interview last week with Adam Grant He was my professor I also saw you speak at the Collaborate conference in 2015, and became a bigger fan after taking your CollabMBA program I also listen to your podcast regularly [Personalize and use emotion]

It would mean a lot to me if you'd be willing to write a blurb for my book, Collapetition, which helps entrepreneurs and business leaders collaborate more effectively [Tailor the correspondence to the person you are addressing It's clear your book is very aligned to Scott's expertise and interests]

You can learn about the book here [Linking more information through a webpage or press kit enables him to decide if he wants to take this on]

Others who agreed to endorse include leaders such as Seth Godin, Sheryl Sandberg, and Reshma Saujani [Exert influence by showing your credibility strategically]

If you agree, I'd be happy to share the manuscript or a couple of chapters with you [Getting consent will make Scott feel valued]

Your endorsement would mean the world to me I hope to hear back from you [Keep the ending short and sweet]

Best,
Christine

When someone asks for help in an authentic, personalized way that makes us feel valued, it's different than when it comes across as all about the person asking. Christine's original email seemed copy-pasted to several people. It was impersonal. It didn't have an authentic tone. So it didn't seem important.

We should know when to shift away from "I" in order to make the other person feel heard. It should feel like an invitation or honor, rather than creating an obligation for the other person.

First ask: What's the goal of my message? What would I consider a successful outcome? Where does it make sense to insert the request? The earlier in the message, the better, as it's only getting harder to capture people's attention. But try not to have more than three to five I's in an email. Write messages that are giving value instead of asking for help or selling something. These days, whenever we receive a message from someone we don't know well, most of us think we're being sold to.

The best way to practice collaboration is to invite, not ask. I started inviting other colleagues to join Poswolsky's program. As it grew, subgroups emerged. I joined one with a few close friends and colleagues, allowing us to connect with each other more closely and regularly.

Suddenly I had hope that my book would be supported well. Growing my own support network—my **solidarity squad**—helped me make the shift from being an isolated "I" to a connected "we"—something almost every author struggles with and can benefit from.

More importantly, my new solidarity squad asked me to do a free webinar about how to build an audience on LinkedIn. I wouldn't have thought of doing such a webinar if they hadn't asked. It turned out to be a huge success, attracting many new partners. I was moving into WE at last.

Key Takeaways:

How Can I Help?
We can measure success by how much impact we have on others—how much we contribute to their success.

The Rise Of Unconventional Partnerships
We should create an ecosystem that has a ripple impact or figure out how we can provide value and fit within an existing ecosystem.

The Niche Community Movement
We gain by building a niche community, starting out small, where we can give value through our unique skills, so each community member stays hungry and connected and helps expand the movement.

Building Our Solidarity Squad
By using curiosity to ask questions, we can understand others better and open doors for collaboration. We can then build a foundation for success by creating a support network to support each other's goals.

"GREAT IDEAS HAPPEN AROUND THE EDGES OF SOCIETY **WHERE THERE'S FLUIDITY AND ELASTICITY.** THE MORE COMPLEX SOCIETY BECOMES, THE MORE WE'RE **THROWN UP WITH NEW CHALLENGES.** THE BEST *ideas* COME WHEN THERE'S FUN —WHEN PEOPLE ENJOY THE PROCESS— WHERE THERE'S DURESS AND STRESS."

- *Jeremy Agnew*, SOCIAL ENTREPRENEUR

"HOW DO WE MARRY **KNOWLEDGE AND WISDOM?** YOUNGER GENERATIONS **HAVE KNOWLEDGE** AND OLDER GENERATIONS **HAVE WISDOM.** HOW DO WE COMBINE THEM **AND EXTRACT THE BEST** VALUE OUT OF THESE TWO?"

- **REUBEN ABOOTORABI**
CEO + FOUNDER, THE AUSTIN AGENCY

"UNDERSTAND WHERE PEOPLE ARE. **FIND OUT WHAT'S GOING ON IN THEIR LIFE.** THE CHALLENGE WE HAVE IS **AS MUCH LINGUISTIC AS IT IS COGNITIVE."**

- MIKE PINO, digital learning + technology strategist.

"WE GET THE BEST IDEAS WHEN WE HAVE A **DIVERSE NETWORK,** EMBRACE AN **OPEN MIND,** AND ARE **INCLUSIVE** WHEN HAVING CONVERSATIONS."

- **THOS GIESKES**, *Managing Director, Oikocredit.*

"THERE IS A NEED FOR A **joined up system** WHERE EVERY PART OF THE **ECOSYSTEM** NEEDS TO WORK **TOGETHER."**

-**BAYO ADELAJA,** CHIEF EXECUTIVE OFFICER, DO IT NOW NOW

"WE NEED RADICAL **collaboration** ACROSS GENERATIONS AS THE KEY INGREDIENT FOR A **SUSTAINABLE FUTURE."**

IRA KAUFMAN
AUTHOR + DIGITAL TRANSFORMATION STRATEGIST

"AN INNOVATION ECOSYSTEM IS A COMPLEX SYSTEM OF **CONNECTIONS AND RELATIONSHIPS** AMONG PEOPLE AND THEIR ENVIRONMENT CALLED RAINFORESTS OR COMPLEX ADAPTIVE SYSTEMS."

Dr. Alistair Brett
CHIEF SCIENTIST, INFYRNO LLC

"AS YOU CONNECT WITH PURPOSE AND BUILD YOUR TRIBE, **IT'S IMPORTANT TO KNOW THAT YOU ARE PART** OF A BIGGER, BROADER, INTERCONNECTED ECOSYSTEM. ACKNOWLEDGING THAT AND PARTICIPATING IN THE ECOSYSTEM **MAY BE VITAL TO YOUR GROWTH AND RESILIENCE."**

- **NEETAL PAREKH,** SOCIAL ENTREPRENEUR + ECOSYSTEM BUILDER

EMPATHY IS THE ENGINE
OF INNOVATION

Chapter 6

Invaluable Empathy

Mastering Human Connection

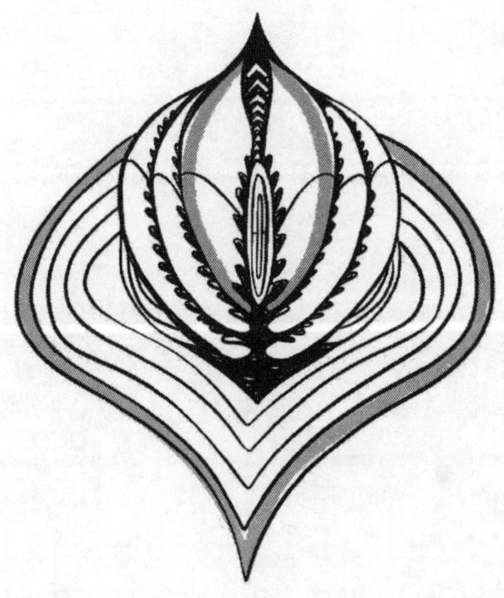

I hosted a dinner at my place for one of my solidarity squads, a group of women foodies. I agonized as they nibbled through my signature goat biryani, tandoori chicken, and samosas. Normally I would love watching them enjoy my food, and telling them all about the trip I had just taken to Liberia. But all I wanted was to get to the end so I could finally share my book outline with non-authors for the first time.

I should have enjoyed the dinner more. They loved the food, and they hated the outline. It was all about ideas that I thought mattered, around innovation and leadership. Honesty is good; collaboration is the thing, right? At that moment, though, it felt it might have been preferable to have a little more empathy on their part for all the work I'd done—stacks of notebooks, piles of sticky notes, pads of flipcharts.

"I wouldn't read this book," one of them said. "It's not original. I've read this stuff before."

"It feels so North American. But you work around the world."

"Who's your audience, anyway? Who actually needs this book?"

"Wouldn't it be better to include other people's viewpoints?"

"Don't worry, Saleema. As Terry Patchett said, the first draft is just you telling yourself the story."

When they went home, I sat alone feeling like crying. I had squeezed in so much hard work scribbling notes on trains from Switzerland to the Netherlands, recording audio notes while sitting by Lake Louise, watching the sunset in the Sahara while. . .pondering my belly button. I thought it was those exotic moments where I'd get the most inspiring insights, but it turned out most of the insights were only interesting to myself.

I was writing a book that no one would read. I was like a failed startup. I felt another lifequake coming on. How could I lack empathy? I had spent so many hours leading workshops on Design Thinking where empathy is the first step.

Right! Empathy is the engine of innovation. It's the first step in Design Thinking for a good reason. To understand what solution people need, we need to understand the people first. How had I overlooked this?

Why Empathy Matters

Empathy is the undervalued stock that enables those who have it to be more successful in many areas than those who lack it.

I recalled a time early in my career in international development when I was tasked to evaluate social development projects in the Dominican Republic. In one project, primary care nurses in the southern region of the island were given laptops and were trained to use an electronic system to record patient information.

But the project was a bust. Everything was fine at first, according to the monitoring reports. They were checking all the boxes. But strong qualitative information wasn't being gathered over time.

The problem was that the team who set up the project had not seen it from the point of view of the people on the ground. The internet didn't work. The nurses didn't understand how to use the computers, even after being trained. The patients wanted face-to-face conversations, not a nurse typing data on a laptop in front of them.

But the project team didn't employ empathy in the monitoring process, so they weren't aware of the nurses' objections. The real problem was that the project team's main goal was to support the Dominican government's need to obtain medical records and data electronically, while the patients' main goal was to get healthy. And the nurses, for obvious reasons, were on the side of the patients ahead of the project.

It was easy for us at that time to criticize the project team's lack of empathy, especially since we were visiting from a developed country. The government actually understood the problem, noting for us that the project was structured to make it impossible to adapt it, leaving no room for empathy to make an impact. There were many factors in the process leading up to this lack of empathy that were far too complicated to just "improve."

This lack of empathy often happens in large projects, where big systems' needs don't allow for easy input from the people concerned. It also happens when we're managing projects that we're not deeply invested in, or where we are far away from the people whom we're supposed to be serving.

Far worse, though, as I found with this very book, this lack of empathy also happens when empathy could more easily be included, because we are in a hurry, or too worried about how we look, or wearing blinders in one of hundreds of possible ways. It's one of the challenges with innovating to solve a problem—we don't understand the problem in the first place.

This is, in fact, why in Design Thinking, the first step to innovate starts with empathy. If not, we would probably never manage to include it, for once the process starts moving it's harder to worry about how it is impacting people. The earlier we bring empathy into any process, the better. Of course, this doesn't mean to skip it if we forgot it earlier, as with this book. Empathy in iteration is also critical—even more so because it is only after you've started that you can evaluate the impact of your work on real people.

Apple is a great example of bringing empathy in early. It wasn't a company founded on empathy originally. But in the early 1980's, when the company was still young, Mike Markkula, one of Apple's first investors, managed to anticipate lessons that were decades away from becoming mainstream. Although design was still a niche profession and Design Thinking hadn't been fully articulated, Markkula wrote "The Apple Marketing Philosophy," a one-page memo stressing three main points. The FIRST point was empathy.

Markkula wrote: "We will truly understand their needs better than any other company."

His goal for Apple was to build an intimate connection with the feelings of the customer. That has been fundamental to the DNA of Apple, and at the source of its success, ever since.

Great design, inspired by Design Thinking methodologies, starts with a deep understanding of the user experience. When we have a high level of empathy for the end user, we can inspire practical creativity. Empathy drives innovative solutions that have an impact.

Empathy is a lot slipperier than it seems. It's easy to criticize others for lacking empathy, but when we do that, we reveal a lack of empathy in ourselves. So how could I up my empathy in time to improve the book? Can empathy even be nurtured, or is it developed during childhood and stuck like that? I knew empathy was important—and yet I was not practicing it. Maybe I didn't understand it as well as I thought.

What Empathy Is And What It Is Not

> "The truth is, rarely can a response make something better. What makes something better is connection."
>
> - Brené Brown, Author of *Dare To Lead*

Amy J. Wilson, author of *Empathy for Change: How to Create a More Understanding World,* is part of the Ripple Impact community. She defines empathy as responding to the thoughts and emotions of others with the purpose of meeting each other's needs.[20] Empathy means truly putting ourselves in someone else's shoes, feeling what they feel, and ensuring they feel heard.

Knowing the definition of empathy doesn't make us master practitioners. Empathy isn't about fixing a problem if the problem is defined on our own terms. To get better at actively practicing empathy, we need to get our empathy skills validated by others. It's not about if we think we hear them, but if THEY feel we hear them. What I thought empathy was, was not empathy at all. This realization led me to create the **What Empathy Is Not** tool.

WHAT EMPATHY IS NOT

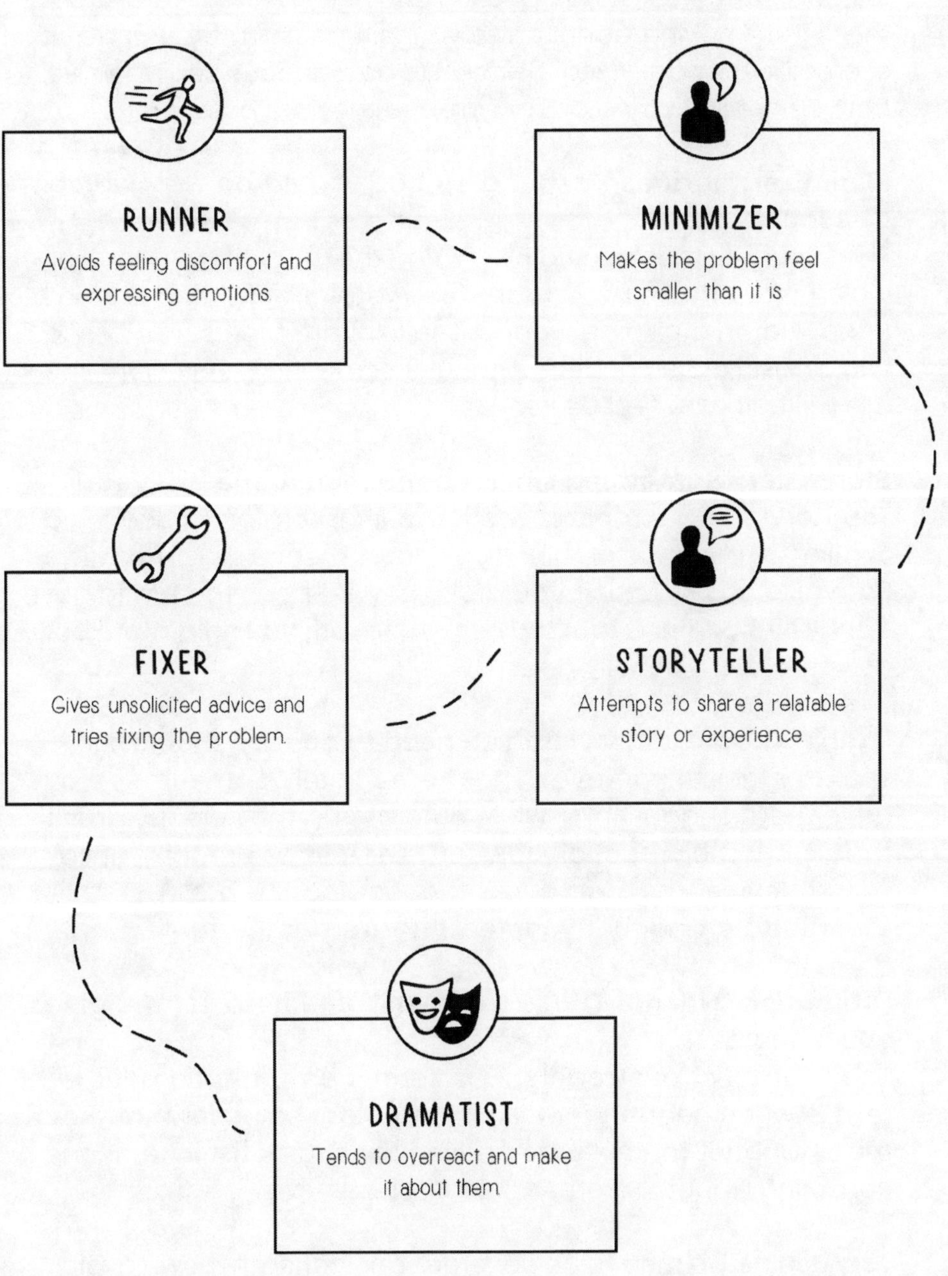

ADAPTED FROM LAURA CLICK, BRAND STRATEGIST

Runner: "Can we pick this up later? I've got an appointment."
The Runner doesn't have enough time or space for you to share fully, and often uses their phone and their calendar to distract them from paying attention to your situation. To the Runner, it seems like they are trying their best to be generous and attentive, but you are just going on and on, and they are busy.

Minimizer: "It doesn't sound so bad. Could be way worse. Cheer up!"
The Minimizer tries to help by making the problem feel smaller, which often makes it actually feel worse, like putting a small Band-Aid on a gaping wound. The Minimizer feels that giving you a positive perspective without first meeting you where you are will help you feel better.

Storyteller: "Something similar happened to me last year!"
The Storyteller attempts to soothe your discomfort by sharing a "similar" experience of their own or of someone they know. The Storyteller thinks letting you know they've "been there and got the T-shirt" conveys that they are there with you right now—but as you know, it usually doesn't.

Fixer: "I know exactly what you need to do. You should. . ."
The Fixer tries to improve things immediately. Sometimes they have great suggestions, while other times, they clearly aren't the expert. Their reaction can come across as preachy, unsolicited advice. The Fixer thinks that solving the problem is all that matters, and that your feelings aren't important.

Dramatist: "Oh, no! That's terrible! Come here, let me give you a hug!"
The Dramatist overreacts. This seems empathetic until we realize when hearing news, they often get so upset that they make it about them. In the end, it's the Dramatist who needs consoling about the other person's bad news.

As much as I've tried to be generous and caring, my own avoidance of empathy actually fit into every one of these categories.

I've been the Runner, too busy giving value to certain people to notice others who might need it more.

The Minimizer is a great tool I've used to empower my Runner—that person's problem isn't worth my time right now, sadly.

I was the Fixer before I was trained as a coach, thinking I would help best by bringing in my expertise and knowledge.

As the Dramatist, I can often get emotional and make things about me, especially if something triggers me emotionally. Some people even call me a drama queen!

And the Storyteller? That's me to a T, of course.

A friend told me a few years back that I was too young and inexperienced to write a book about my life. Now I realized he was wrong. I needed to start showing empathy not just for this book and its future readers, but also for myself. Why was I putting all this pressure on being the source of everything?

I had embarked on a 100 Coffee Challenge to get out of my lifequake. Now, I would embark on a 100 Interview Challenge to avoid myself—and my book—having another one. It was time to stop writing and talking, and start asking and listening.

Don't Just Talk, Act

How we see ourselves is often very different from how others see us.

"Most designers look like sexy Ferraris. They wear skinny jeans and sexy tennis shoes. And then I come in looking like a Ford truck. I'm simple, I'm common,

there's nothing special about that.
I wear Ariat jeans, vests, and boots."

- Michael Brown, former Chief Experience Officer at DICK'S Sporting Goods

Michael Brown told me that for several years he wore cowboy boots every day, the complete antithesis of what people expected in design culture. He'd ask every audience he spoke to if they liked his boots and emphasized that he wanted their honest opinion. On average, ninety-five percent of people said they liked his boots. Then he'd ask: "Do you want to buy my boots? I'm sponsored by Ariat and I have to show that I sold fifty of these this year."

He conducted this experiment around the world, and the results were consistent: not a single person has bought his boots.

"People will tell me what they think I want to hear," Brown points out. "But it's not their true belief."

What Brown means is that understanding ourselves through the lens of others is essential, like we discussed in Chapter 1. Will people just compliment our boots? Or will they actually buy our boots?

What people value is often different from what they say they value. When we see that people don't value who we think we are, we put on a new mask. We'll exchange our boots for Nike Air Force Ones if we think this will help them validate us.

To figure out what my future readers wanted, I decided to do some **Empathy Mapping.**

EMPATHY MAPPING

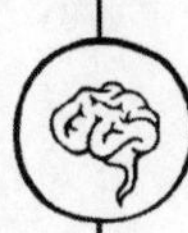

WHAT DO THEY THINK AND FEEL?

what really counts
major preoccupations
worries and aspirations

WHAT DO THEY SEE?

environment
friends
what the market offers

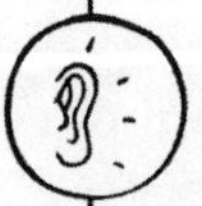

WHAT DO THEY HEAR?

what friends say
what boss says
what influencers say

WHAT DO THEY SAY AND DO?

attitude in public
appearance
behavior toward others

PAIN

fears
frustrations
obstacles

GAIN

wants
needs
measures of succes

ADAPTED FROM XPLANE

Here's how Empathy Mapping works:

- Place observations about what people think and feel, see, hear, and say and do, into their respective boxes.
- List their pros and cons at the bottom.
- After writing in each box, take a step back and look at the map as a whole.
- What insights or conclusions can we draw?
- What seems new or surprising?
- What unexpected patterns do we notice?
- Are there any contradictions between or within the boxes?
- What human needs emerge?

We gather information directly from the audience we're trying to understand. By diving into what people say, do, think, and feel, we can gain clarity on what it's like to walk in their boots.

My potential book audience saw me differently than I saw myself, and I resisted this until I saw how important their perspectives are. As writers, we need to see ourselves through the lens of our audience. Others can see us better than we see ourselves.

Empathy Is An Activity, Not A Position

We need to understand a problem through the lens of those experiencing it when we are seeking solutions.

It was sunny, hot, and sticky. People stared at us as if they hadn't seen foreigners before. Half of our team was sick with heat stroke, but we kept plowing through.

We were in a small town outside of Monrovia, Liberia, facilitating a focus group with the local community in a gazebo adjacent to the town hall. The community was being negatively impacted by a road construction project that aimed to bring economic opportunities while increasing accessibility. The accident rate was high because the community lacked awareness of the construction dangers and the project provided inadequate supervision. We were a small team of intrapreneurs that had been awarded a youth innovation grant by an international organization to solve this problem.

We first had to understand the big picture. We interviewed each of the stakeholders and ran focus groups so we could better understand the issues. We quickly saw that every group of stakeholders—the Chinese road contractors, the Liberian government, and the community itself—had very different perspectives. How could we get this diverse and seemingly incompatible mix of people to see eye-to-eye when we brought them together for the Design Thinking workshop?

Our team incorporated a lot of team building activities over the two days to maximize empathy while overcoming the language barriers and cultural differences. As a result, we all ended up dancing, laughing, and having a lot of fun throughout the workshop. By the end, we came to a consensus about the road project, and the groups worked together over the next few months to solve the problem.

The interviews and team building were a form of active and intentional empathy that helped us synchronize a disparate group to innovate together.

I thought back to that experience and realized it could help me with *Innovation Starts With I.* I brought the following principles we learned in Liberia into my 100 book interviews:

- Brainstorm, refine, and order questions by themes or subject areas to structure the interview flow
- Make eye contact and match the postural height of your interviewee
- Introduce yourself and establish a conversational tone
- Dig for meaning and follow up
- Keep asking why until you get a substantive answer
- Don't ask loaded questions or suggest answers—ask open-ended questions
- Encourage stories
- Allow the conversation to deviate from your plan and follow unexpected threads
- Don't speak for more than 25 percent of the airtime
- Interview for at least twenty to sixty minutes to get rich data
- Silence can be helpful: interviewees may fill the void with interesting, new insights
- Observe nonverbal cues
- Document the interview by recording or audio transcribing it

Mastering The Underrated Skill Of Listening

"Leadership lives in listening. You can't just make assumptions or listen to respond, because then you're just listening to you, and your judgments and assessments of what the other person is saying, instead of actually what the other person is saying."

- Michael Saloio, Serial Entrepreneur

Listening is foundational to building empathy. I've been lousy at listening all my life. Most of us aren't very good at it. It's too easy to start thinking of a response while the other person is talking. If we instead ask people curious questions, they will tell us what matters to them. Saloio says that leadership lives in listening. He says that if we're listening to others through the lens of "Already Always Listening,"[21] our assumptions get in the way of the other person's words, and we hear what we're thinking, not what they're saying: "You're listening to you, and your judgments and assessments."

Here are the **Four Levels of Listening** from shallow to deep.

THE 4 LEVELS OF LISTENING

LEVEL 1

SELF LISTENING

This form of listening is the most common. Instead of really listening, we are thinking about how someone's words are impacting us and already formulating a response before the other person finishes talking.

WHAT ARE MY THOUGHTS?

LEVEL 2

FACTS LISTENING

We're simply hearing what the other person is saying. This is when we're listening to the content of what is being said and absorbing the information. We can usually repeat what they said. We may or may not have tapped into the other person's feelings.

WHAT ARE THEY LITERALLY SAYING?

LEVEL 3

EMPATHIC LISTENING

We're listening for the feelings that are being expressed and trying to adapt reactively. We may or may not be paying close attention to the actual content of what is being said. Sometimes, there is a disconnect between what is being said in words and the demeanors and feelings being expressed.

WHAT EMOTIONS ARE THEY EXPRESSING?

LEVEL 4

COLLABORATIVE LISTENING

This is the most connected form of listening. Here we're listening with curiosity and openness. For some, this type of listening comes naturally, especially those with a high degree of intuition, whereas, for others, it takes practice and awareness to get here.

WHAT ARE THEIR UNSPOKEN WORDS?

When we're practicing **Self Listening** and **Facts Listening**, we don't help those around us actually feel heard. We should continuously work on improving our **Empathic Listening** and **Collaborative Listening**.

I'd like to say more about listening, but I don't consider myself a very good listener yet. I do all right listening to people who are similar to me, but if I don't empathize with someone easily, I struggle to really understand them.

Identifying And Captivating Our Audience

Our ability to influence accelerates when we amplify others.

As I started listening in my interviews, I realized more and more clearly that the topics I wanted to cover in this book would be best suited to be read by entrepreneurs, not innovation professionals.

We need to distinguish our audience in a different way than we think. It's not about who we want to speak to. It's about who wants to listen to us. As I started to pay better attention, I realized that my primary audience looks a lot like who I was not too long ago.

Whose pain points can we address best? Who can we help become successful while leveraging our sweet spot? Who empathizes with us?

We may have to test out a variety of audiences to find the right one. And as we evolve, our audience will also evolve. This is why building and maintaining a personal brand is so important. People will remember how WE make them feel, not how our company makes them feel.

After the 100 interviews, I ended up with a completely new book outline. Which meant I had to rewrite this book from scratch. You've read this far, so I think my breakthrough in empathy has helped.

Key Takeaways:

Why Empathy Matters
Empathy inspires creativity and innovation.

What Empathy Is And What It Is Not
We're being empathetic when we are meeting others' needs and ensuring they feel heard. Understanding what empathy is not can help strengthen our empathy muscle.

Don't Just Talk, Act
Self-awareness is key to developing empathy.

Empathy Is An Activity, Not A Position
When interacting with others, we allow ourselves to deviate from the plan and keep digging for insights to maximize curiosity and allow empathy to arise.

Mastering The Underrated Skill Of Listening
The more we practice our listening skills, the stronger our empathy becomes, and the more likely we'll innovate.

Identifying And Captivating Our Audience
We benefit by testing out a variety of audiences to understand the ones we can best serve. How we see ourselves may be very different than how others see us.

"**EMPATHY** IS SOMETHING YOU LEARN THROUGH MULTIPLE TOUCHPOINTS IN YOUR LIFE. YOU LEARN EMPATHY FROM THE WORK YOU DO, TO THE LESSONS PASSED DOWN TO YOU THROUGH FAMILY, TO WHAT IS HAPPENING IN THE WORLD AROUND YOU. IT'S ALL ABOUT HOW AWARE YOU ARE OF WHAT'S GOING ON OUTSIDE OF YOUR OWN BUBBLE."
- DIYA KHANNA, DIVERSITY + INCLUSION LEADER, AMAZON

"I WANT TO RECRUIT A TEAM AROUND ME THAT ARE GIVERS. **EVEN SMALL GIVES ARE REALLY IMPACTFUL.**"
- ANGELA SPECHT, VACCINE ACCESS STRATEGY + IMPACT LEADER, JOHNSON & JOHNSON

"**ACKNOWLEDGEMENT AND TRANSPARENCY ARE AN IMPORTANT PART OF EMPATHY.** TELL SOMEONE SOMETHING THEY DON'T WANT TO HEAR BUT DO IT IN A WAY THAT'S NOT PERSONAL."
- DESMOND SMITH, CHIEF CUSTOMER OFFICER, FANNIE MAE

"PEOPLE DON'T NEED TO WEAR DIAPERS AGAIN BUT **EMPATHY** GOES BACK TO CHILDHOOD AND CONNECTING TO YOUR INNER CHILD."
- PIETER SPINDER
AUTHOR, FROM FEAR TO FREEDOM

"**- EMPATHY -** IS HARD TO MEASURE. **- IMPACT -** IS A TOUCHPOINT TO SHIFT THAT CONVERSATION."
- COREY PONDER, FOUNDER, EM|PACT STRATEGIES

"WE ARE A DEEPLY LONELY COUNTRY IN NEED OF **HUMAN CONNECTION** THAT HASN'T CRACKED THE CODE ON WHERE OR HOW TO FIND IT. AS YOU GO THROUGH AND **BUILD EMPATHY** FOR YOURSELF AND OTHERS, TAKE NOTE THAT TRUST IS EARNED IN DROPLETS, AND LOST IN BUCKETS."
- AMY J. WILSON, AUTHOR + EMPATHY LEADER

"THE WORLD IS BECOMING RELIANT ON **EMPATHY**. YOU CAN'T IGNORE WHAT PEOPLE THINK AND YOU CAN'T SELL THINGS AT THEM WITHOUT SELLING IT WITH THEM."
- Aiman Kabli, Author + Entrepreneur

INFLUENCE IS THE OUTCOME
OF BEING AUTHENTIC

Chapter 7

Inspiring Authenticity

Expressing Our Exponential Selves

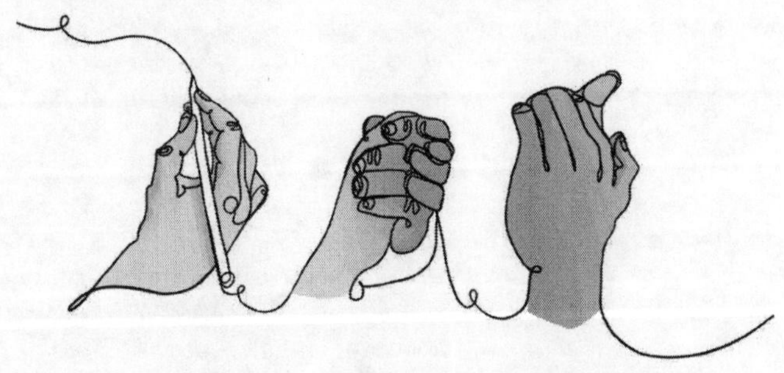

"Saleema, I think you should be more authentic when you post online. All you do is talk about your successes. It's kind of like the book chapters you've shown me so far. Where are you in all of this? The real you?"

I took a deep breath. My best friend was right. But why would I want to share about my failures? Who would want to hear about that?

"What's something you don't ever share with anyone?"

It was an easy question to answer. "My mother's death. It's a huge part of who I am, and why I am the way I am. But I'm not looking to hold a pity party."

"Stop worrying what others think. Do what's authentic for you."

3:46

Yesterday marked 16 years since I lost my mother, which is half a life ago seeing she passed shortly after my 16th birthday. Until now, I've never written about my loss online as I didn't have the courage to share what I went through.

As a child, I thought I would always have the nuclear family I had enjoyed until my mum was diagnosed with breast cancer when I was 12 years old. Seeing her go through remission with all her hope and strength and then get diagnosed with lung cancer shortly after was even harder. Sometimes, we need that little light in the tunnel to help us develop the strength for bigger adversities.

Though I had lost several family members prior to losing my mum, I didn't know how to deal with her being gone. When I saw her pass, I felt numb and couldn't even cry—as much as that logically seemed like the right thing to do. Part of me felt relieved that she was no longer suffering, part of me was in shock as to how I would live without her, and part of me kept asking "Why me?" as I was surrounded by my friends/family and many of their so-called "nuclear families".

We all have our own way of dealing with loss. For me, I embarked on living around the world for several years on a mission to find a "home" and to feel loved and accepted. Through my experiences, I realized that home starts from having peace within myself.

Whenever I reflect back, I realize how much adversities truly make us emotionally resilient. Oftentimes, we're conditioned to see things as black and white, bad or good. Everything is interconnected, and we should truly embrace our adversities because they are part of who we are, part of our story.

I realize more and more that I have a lot of my mum within myself and carry many of her gifts, even though I didn't get to know her as an adult.

Sometimes things happen and it doesn't make sense at the moment, but everything falls into place later. Life is full of ebbs and flows.

I'm grateful to everyone that has been there for me throughout the journey of life.

I still can't believe I hit the POST button. A few minutes later, a friend called me and told me to take it down! But I ignored him. The post got nearly 500 likes—the most likes I had ever gotten on a post. It wasn't a post that I wanted anyone to like. I just posted it.

What we most hold back from sharing is often exactly what others want to hear. I understood that what seems self-centered is often the most generous. And I realized that in order to write this book, I needed to be more authentic. Did that mean I just had to spill my guts? Who would want to read that?

Authenticity Is The Source Of Trust

"Vulnerability is the birthplace of love, belonging, joy, courage, empathy, and creativity. It is the source of hope, empathy, accountability, and authenticity."

- Brené Brown, Author of *Dare To Lead*

In the old days, we could fake authenticity. When the Internet was newer, a lot of us used stage names. I ran businesses for years without my clients seeing me. We exchanged emails. We didn't have video calls. My photo was nowhere to be found online. I didn't post on social.

But the world has evolved. These days, people care less about the content and more about the authenticity of the person delivering it.

There's so much noise now. How do we know what to filter out? We do quick and aggressive due diligence: Is this person who they say they are? Do they feel genuine?

The bar was raised even higher by the pandemic. Video calls became mandatory. Humans became desperate for connection. The requirements for trust skyrocketed. We want to see potential clients and job candidates, even if just on Zoom. We almost forget they are interviewing us too. And the more we trust them, the more they trust us.

My post about my mother increased my courage to proceed with this book, so I continued using the same technique. I shared stories on social media about my book journey. I turned my frameworks into graphics and posts.

As my friend had predicted, the biggest impact came when I shared my personal story, instead of career topics. My followers found me more interesting than information. Posts about struggling to market myself went viral. Aspiring speakers sent DMs expressing their gratitude and sharing stories of their own rejections. Authenticity was lighting a fire.

I thought back to when I co-launched a digital marketing agency. We were recognized in our first year as the fastest-growing agency in our industry. But we also failed fast. Our clients who came in with a solid customer base continued to thrive, but the earlier-stage ones didn't grow. Yet these young companies were the ones we had been most passionate to help. Challenging, yes, but with the most potential for greatest impact.

Why? Our articles were well-researched. Our topics were catchy. Our information was useful. What went wrong?

Our content lacked authenticity. There wasn't a personality behind it. No emotions. No humanity. It was professional and sharp. But it felt mechanistic.

We were knowledgeable about many niches, but we weren't experts. We didn't live in the worlds of our clients day in and day out. We weren't serving their customers. We couldn't speak in their voices. We weren't them and we didn't know them well enough.

Trust is the gateway to influence. To succeed in today's digital world, we need to double down on building trust with our customers. Eighty-six percent of consumers say that authenticity is important when deciding what brands they like and support. More than half of consumers think that less than half of brands create content that resonates as authentic.[22]

Authenticity isn't just important after the customer gets to know you. It's essential at the top of the funnel. At the awareness stage of **The Customer Journey**, when just beginning to engage with our audience, our leads will only move to considering working with us when they see us as authentic in the first interactions. Authenticity is the first step to credibility and influence. This is why sharing success stories is so important.

THE CUSTOMER JOURNEY

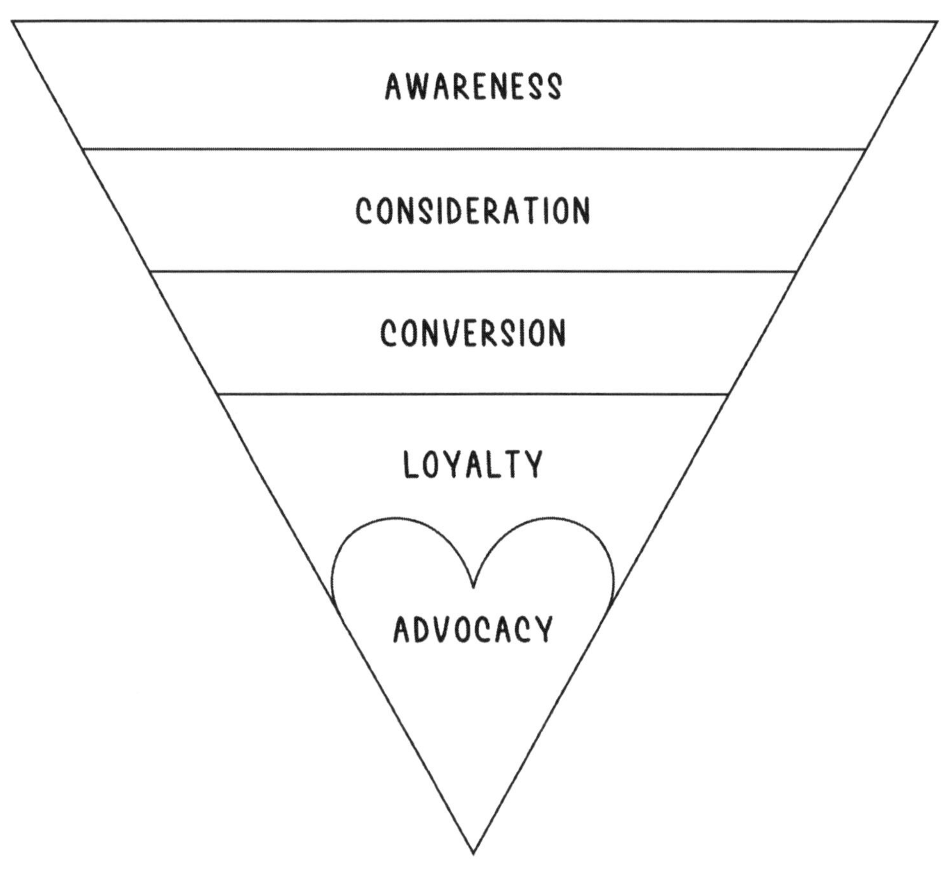

We Not Me: Authenticity Through Relationship

"Authenticity without empathy is selfish. Authenticity is not just about expressing our own thoughts and feelings—it's about conveying our respect for others."

- Adam Grant, Author of *Think Again*

As my team and I began to interview entrepreneurs to understand their needs for this book, we noticed a disturbing pattern. When we asked them a simple question about what their business goals were, these were the kinds of answers we heard.

"To earn $10,000 every month in my first year of launching."

"To gain one million followers in the next nine months."

"To be my own boss and retire by the age of 40."

Me me me me me. And that was what they said when we asked them to be authentic.

We often think that being authentic means being honest about ourselves. That's part of it. But what that tends to make us do is think of the problem I am trying to solve for *us*. This is okay for a start, especially during personal reinvention. But it won't help us have an authentic impact outside of ourselves. To do this, we need to expand our authenticity to think of the communities around us.

When we ask entrepreneurs "Why?" a dozen times and get them to rephrase their needs in terms of WE—the answers come out as far more powerful:

"To build a team so we can make an exponential impact together."

"To help X number of people become successful."

"To help cancer survivors share their stories so they can inspire cancer patients."

The next step in building authenticity is to take the WE vision and apply it to reality. How did we get where we are? We keep drilling down until we get to discomfort. HOW WE GOT HERE is what makes each of us as unique as our fingerprints and retinas:

"I grew up in poverty and had to work hard. I want to help others lift themselves up."

"I spent years failing to make a difference in a big corporation. I want to build a movement of innovators in human resources."

"I lost everything to get over my cancer, but I'm healthy now. I want others to see that they too can triumph and live long and healthy lives."

Sara Ness, Founder and CEO of Authentic Revolution, talks about the importance of knowing ourselves in order to authentically connect with others. When we're aware of all the layers of our being—our desires, our motivations, our deeper truths—we can speak from places that cultivate empathy since others know what it's like to feel as we do: "the only way out is through."

Ness adds that when we operate at the **Surface Level** we end up disconnected. It's easy to blame others for our own feelings. "Hey! You upset me! You should have told me you were going to do that!"

It may be uncomfortable to take responsibility, but it's authentic and leads to better connections. Operating at the **Authentic Level** ties us to other people. "I feel upset. I lose my confidence when people don't support me enough. Please, I need you to be more supportive if you could."

Instead of attacking the other person's views, Ness suggests that we are better off asking them open questions. Seeing their world through our own eyes gives no space for a conversation. We must listen from their perspective. What are they *not* saying? How can we invite them to share the unsaid words?

As Ness points out: "One of us has to be brave enough to take the bandage off."

More vulnerable equals more human.

We begin to understand ourselves better when we grasp the emotional states of others. When we spend time with each other and have meaningful conversations, we realize that we are more similar than we think. Chances are that the other person has no idea how you're feeling—unless you share authentically.

Despite technological advances, business continues to be a game of relationships. The combination of authenticity and empathy allows us to identify key pain points that drive innovative ideas. By leveraging the "I" to prioritize the impact we want to have on others, we're able to get closer to achieving our vision. Here are some questions to reflect on before having a conversation.

THE 5 W's TO PRIME OURSELVES FOR AUTHENTIC CONVERSATIONS

WHO Who do you think you have to be around this person?
Who do you think they expect you to be?

WHAT What emotion are you currently feeling towards the situation?
What concept do you have of yourself at this very moment?

WHERE What's the context?
What do you know about this person culturally?

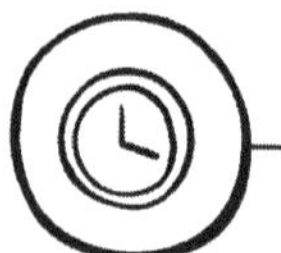

WHEN What's the timing like?
What are they currently going through?

WHY Why are you interacting?
Why do you care about this connection?

The Paradox Of Authenticity: The Exponential Self

"Global change is contributing to an amplified sense of the importance of self."

- Rohit Bhargava, Trend Curator and Author of *Megatrends*

Research[23] indicates that individualism has increased by about twelve percent worldwide since 1960. Only four countries—Cameroon, Malawi, Malaysia, and Mali—showed a substantial decrease in individualistic practices over time, while thirty-four out of forty-one countries showed a notable increase. And only five countries—Armenia, China, Croatia, Ukraine, and Uruguay—showed a substantial decrease in individualistic values over time, with thirty-nine out of fifty-three countries showing a substantial increase.

We're living in an I-focused world. We feel the desire to express our individuality more and more. But is it confidence? Or narcissism? Some people say that social media and selfies enable us to express our authentic, unique identities, while others say that social media and selfies have led to entitlement and insecurity.[24]

Either way, the rise in individualism on digital platforms is driving us to think more about how we present ourselves, especially virtually. Bhargava calls this trend "amplified identity," as our LinkedIn profiles, Tweets, social media profiles, online dating profiles, and selfies—our online identities—are the ultimate expression of who we are. Or rather, "a carefully crafted self-portrait" of our different digital personas. Bhargava adds: "when our sense of self is outsized, we may become more narcissistic, more targeted for criticism, and more vulnerable to co-opting our identities."[25]

"We often show up at least one layer above who we really are. We don't express our true selves when we communicate with others."

- Sara Ness

I call this trend **The Exponential Self**, because it enables us to more easily share ourselves, our thoughts, and our stories. We should not view these different digital identities as in conflict, but rather as an opportunity to connect with different audiences. What we say and who we show up as on LinkedIn, Facebook, and Instagram are not the same. We are evolving into different versions of ourselves faster than ever before. In this Reinvention Revolution, experimenting and testing different types of content with different audiences enables us to evolve into who we're becoming.

THE EXPONENTIAL SELF

LINKEDIN

FACEBOOK

INSTAGRAM

CLUBHOUSE

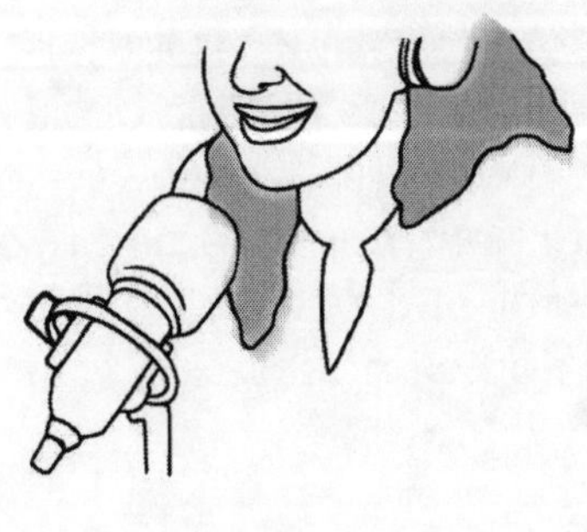

We might use Instagram to share our personal life and our vacation photos. On LinkedIn, we'll be more professional and formal. Although these lines shift and blur, it's critical to understand the personas we are presenting on each platform. All of them still need to be authentic.

But authenticity doesn't mean just being there as whatever you happen to be. Authenticity can be intentional and conscious. Authenticity doesn't come from just saying what's on our mind first. Our first draft is often just bad, not authentic.

It can help to think about who we see as successful and model our own path on theirs in some way. For example, I think of Tim Ferriss, who inspired me to leverage freelance talent when I started my translation business. I think of Leila Janah, who inspired me to build a personal brand after hiding behind the scenes. Of Gary Vaynerchuk, who inspired me to create content. Of Simon Sinek, who inspired me to ask "why" whenever starting something. Of all the family, friends, and colleagues that surrounded me. Of my brother—you remember how much he helped me.

Who do we admire? Why? What characteristics do we share? What traits can we strengthen?

We can practice authenticity better by testing and iterating, because it's not just about sharing "honestly." It's about sharing in a way that empowers others. When we're thoughtful about our community in a non-obvious way, even what seems like a small effort can help foster an authentic connection that has a ripple impact.

Behind The Scenes: The Journey Not The Destination

People don't want to hear about success. They want to hear about the journey. But success isn't the destination OR the journey—it's the lessons learned along the way.

A colleague sent an email asking for tips on how to become a speaker at INBOUND, a leading annual business and marketing conference hosted by HubSpot where he had seen me speak. I began drafting a response to him, and it just kept flowing. I didn't just write about how I did it myself the one time—but also how I had failed to achieve it in other years. I shared the entire story from start to finish.

It got so long and authentic I decided to turn it into a blog post. I was proud of myself for sharing my failures. By telling the whole story, not just the happy ending, the post checked the boxes of the Great Idea Framework: non-obvious, concrete, timely, and useful!

I'd never posted content on marketing. I was worried it would reduce the impact of my successes because people would see them as something I'd gained through marketing rather than skill and merit.

But if I could share about my mother, certainly I could share about this. And the post got traction. I decided to share my book struggles. People liked the insider stories of the unfinished product. They especially liked hearing about the failures.

It's a lot easier for us to relate with someone's failures than their successes because we only succeed once after dozens or thousands of microsteps!

As soon as I repositioned myself to express who I am right now instead of who I thought everyone needed to see me as, my platform took off. Every post. People started commenting on my content. They shared suggestions for this book. They offered introductions and media opportunities. In place of a sad saga of stressful isolation to overcome, my book journey became the catalyst for an engaged community that drove me to finish the manuscript.

Empathy drove my authenticity, and authenticity was now driving public empathy. What a cycle!

Key Takeaways:

Authenticity Is The Source Of Trust
By developing authenticity, we cultivate strong trust with our community and turn them into customers.

We Not Me: Authenticity Through Relationship
Leaning into our discomfort and practicing vulnerability with others enable us to move from surface level to authentic conversations.

The Paradox Of Authenticity: The Exponential Self
Expressing our exponential self authentically across different platforms enables us to better connect to our audiences.

Behind The Scenes: The Journey Not The Destination
Sharing our stories as full processes—the good, the bad, and the ugly—is more intriguing and valuable than sharing our successes. In fact, stories of the "ugly"—our failures and how we overcame them—are the most authentic and compelling of all.

"*Influence* IS A BYPRODUCT OF BEING **HONEST AND AUTHENTIC** AND TAKING ACTION ALIGNED WITH THAT WAY OF BEING."
- ELENI PALLAS, EXECUTIVE COACH + ORGANIZATIONAL ACTIVIST

"*In order to influence,* WE HAVE TO START WITH OURSELVES. **WE HAVE TO UNDERSTAND OURSELVES** THROUGH *self-reflection* AND HOW WE'RE SHOWING UP AS HUMAN BEINGS, AS LEADERS. **OUR VALUES ARE DYNAMIC AND OUR AUTHENTICITY EVOLVES.**"
- TORIAN RICHARDSON, GLOBAL DIVERSITY RECRUITING LEADER, NVIDIA

"AS WE AGE, WE GO THROUGH EXPERIENCES AND INSERT OURSELVES INTO SYSTEMS THAT **IMPACT OUR LEVEL OF AUTHENTICITY AND HOW WE PRACTICE IT**. WHEN WE SEE HOW WE'RE EXISTING WITHIN SOCIETY, OUR AUTHENTICITY CAN FLOW LIKE A DAM. IT COMES AND GOES, EBBS AND FLOWS, IT'S NOT A CONSISTENT STREAM OR SWITCH BUT RATHER MORE OF A SPECTRUM."
- DIYA KHANNA, DIVERSITY + INCLUSION LEADER, AMAZON

"THERE ARE TWO SUBSETS OF AUTHENTICITY: **AWARENESS AND CONGRUENCE.** AWARENESS OF WHAT'S HAPPENING INSIDE OF ME WHILE CONGRUENCE IN WHAT'S HAPPENING IN THE OUTER WORLD, IN HOW ONE THINKS, FEELS, AND SAYS. **WHAT LANGUAGES DO THEY SPEAK? HOW DO PEOPLE COMMUNICATE BEST? HOW DO THEY PROCESS?** WE EXPECT PEOPLE TO RELATE RELATIVELY THE SAME BUT THEY DON'T."
- **SARA NESS**, CHIEF INSTIGATOR, AUTHENTIC REVOLUTION

"**AUTHENTICITY** WITHOUT EMPATHY **IS SELFISH.** AUTHENTICITY WITHOUT BOUNDARIES **IS CARELESS.** BE TRUE TO YOUR VALUES, **BUT SHOW REGARD** FOR OTHERS' VALUES."
- *Adam Grant*
AUTHOR + WHARTON SCHOOL PROFESSOR

"**PEOPLE INFLUENCE** MORE THROUGH THEIR *behavior* THAN THROUGH THEIR *words*. YOU HAVE TO PRACTICE WHAT YOU PREACH THROUGH YOUR OWN BEHAVIOR.
- **ALEX FERNANDEZ-GARITA**
CORPORATE SOCIAL RESPONSIBILITY LEADER, JOHNSON & JOHNSON

"PEOPLE DON'T BECOME SUPERFANS THE MOMENT THEY FIND YOU. THEY BECOME SUPERFANS BECAUSE OF THE **MAGICAL MOMENTS** YOU CREATE FOR THEM OVER TIME."
- PAT FLYNN, AUTHOR + ENTREPRENEUR

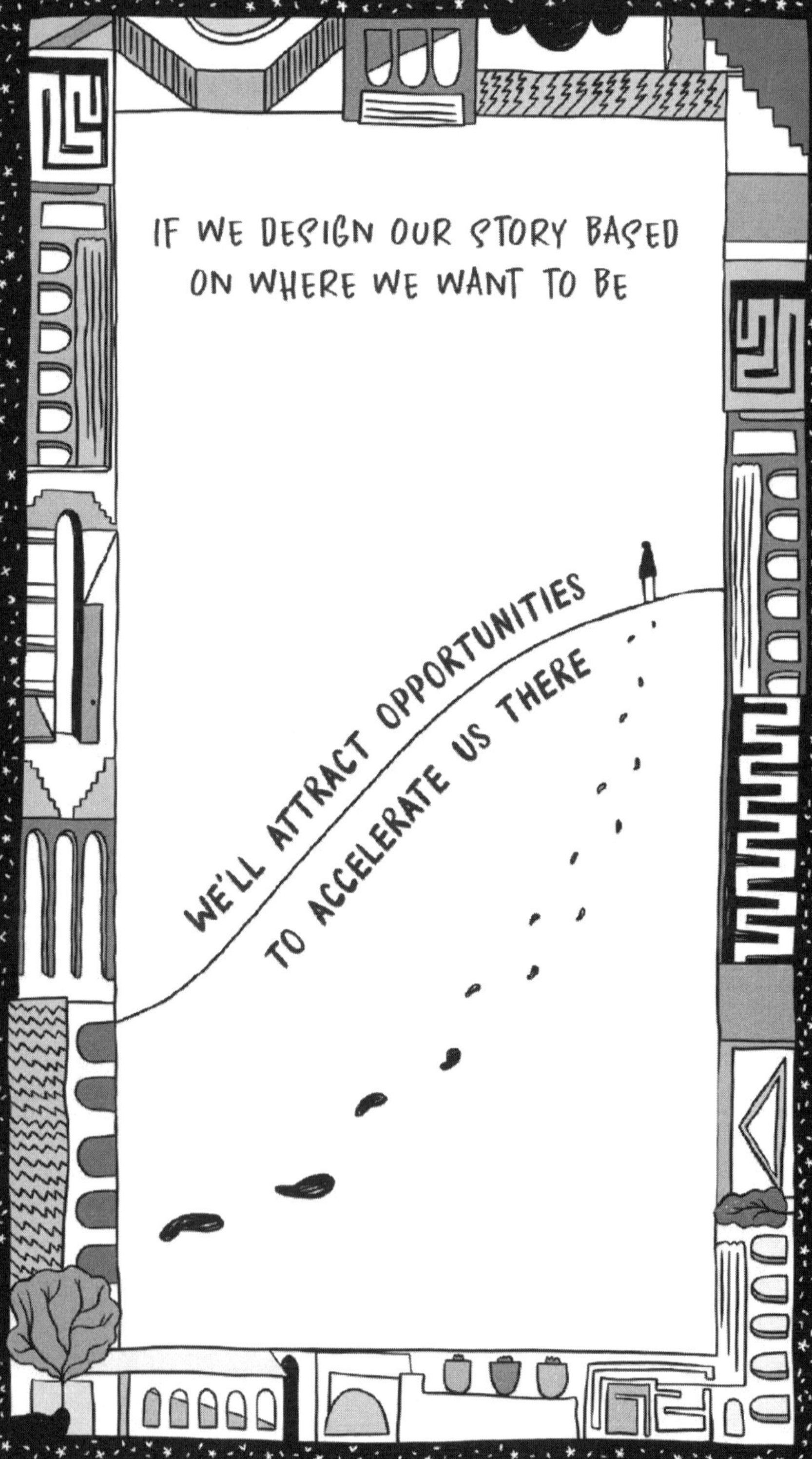

IF WE DESIGN OUR STORY BASED
ON WHERE WE WANT TO BE
WE'LL ATTRACT OPPORTUNITIES
TO ACCELERATE US THERE

Chapter 8

Impactful Storytelling

Designing Our Stories

After I finished the new draft of this book, I felt stuck. I wanted to express myself as "we" but it wasn't working. I decided to put the book aside for a while and go back to public speaking, hoping this would inspire me to create a better third draft.

I must have been getting better at listening to myself, because the strategy worked quickly. I gave a talk during Global Entrepreneurship Week and a storytelling coach, Gbenga Ogunjimi, attended the event. I knew him well. He was the friend I had shared my entrepreneurial journey with shortly after moving to the United States when I was in the middle of my lifequake.

I told him about what I had been up to, my reinvention journey, and my book struggles. He asked if I would like him to share his thoughts. I couldn't believe what came out of his mouth.

"Saleema 3.0 is an entrepreneur who uses her superpower to scale up businesses. To take their ideas and products to make millions of dollars and create immense value in a short time. She uses her skills in sales, marketing, and storytelling to identify, create, and distribute wealth. She likes spending time in the community, helping minorities, especially women

of color, to be better leaders. Corporations hire her to speak to their leadership team not only to unlock the wealth in their product, but also to unlock the wealth in their people. It's this Saleema 3.0 that you need to talk about. Who cares about the old ones?"

Gbenga was giving me the key to moving forward—telling my future story instead of my past one. And not the story I would have told alone, but the story we were telling collaboratively. He had listened carefully and was speaking back to me what I was trying to create but was too timid to say clearly myself.

Storytelling, Gbenga was saying, is also about designing the stories we need to live tomorrow so we can position ourselves to attract opportunities that will accelerate us onward. I had to reconsider my story as Saleema 3.0—before I was even living as Saleema 3.0. Okay, I could see it was true—but how could I adopt it?

The Ripple Impact Of Storytelling

Who we tell our stories to and how we tell them can make all the difference.

I was sitting in my cubicle when I received the email. I was a year and a half into my job at the Inter-American Development Bank. Work was frustrating. Management was dismissing all of my ideas. My boss was declining opportunities colleagues offered to work on interesting projects around Latin America. I had just graduated from two brutal years of studying international economics and my boss wanted me to focus on communications work, which I didn't yet know was one of my sweet spots. This was almost a decade ago.

Ah yes, the email. My classmate was promoting a weekend business bootcamp. It got my attention. I needed inspiration. Spending $200 on an event was a big deal for me at the time. I wasn't used to investing in myself. And I had never labeled myself an "entrepreneur." I was an entrepreneur in Brazil and Italy out of accident, desperation, and necessity. I wasn't aware of startup ecosystems. I had no clue what VCs or angel investors were. I'd never had a mentor. I'd never attended a "networking event" or "conference." So I had no idea what to expect. But my gut told me to go for it.

We spent the weekend learning about Lean Startup and "getting out of the building" to validate our ideas, which meant we went to the streets and asked businesses if they were interested in our product.

During the 2009 financial crisis, being an entrepreneur meant I couldn't get a job. This workshop was four years later, and I was still ashamed to talk about my translation business, thinking of it as a failure in the conventional sense.

Towards the end of our workshop, one speaker, Libby Tucker, promised to teach us how to live anywhere in the world and run our business using her company's platform, Elance. By hiring freelancers remotely, she said, we could grow our business without breaking our budget.

Elance was the platform that saved me in Italy. It felt like my insides were jumping up and down. My inner voice was screaming at me to go up and talk to her. But I was terrified of speaking in public. There was no way I would say anything in front of all these people.

She was mobbed after the presentation. I wasn't as confident as the other entrepreneurs there or as bold as they were in demanding attention. So I waited until everyone else was finished, took a couple of deep breaths, and stepped forward. My Italian story gushed out of me.

I was surprised when she asked to interview me as a testimonial. I was even more shocked when, after I said yes, she pulled out her phone and started to record me. You mean, right now?

Other participants started gathering around, enjoying my story. I found it surprisingly easy to share. I had never told the whole adventure to anybody other than Gbenga. Telling it that day changed my life. I was sharing authentically to total strangers for the first time.

We tell our most powerful stories when we are being authentic.

A few months later, Libby contacted me to offer me a part-time job to become a brand evangelist for Elance, which has since become Upwork. I would be the lead for the Washington, D.C. area. She wanted me to keep telling my story to potential customers, to train entrepreneurs to build remote teams, to run startup events, and to help manage Elance's local partnership with WeWork, the coworking space that was about to launch.

It was a detour from my career plans, and I had never felt so excited. I worked on lunch breaks, evenings, and weekends. This side hustle made me perform better, not worse, in my day job. It also helped my day job organization directly, as I taught them to use the platform to hire remote talent. Sourcing translators and designers this way saved them time, money, and headaches.

Several months later, I was running a multimedia storytelling campaign at WeWork and met a serial entrepreneur who struck a chord with me. He was twenty-three years old, and extremely smart. He offered me a job and the opportunity to co-found the digital marketing agency I shared about earlier. A ripple impact of going to the first workshop, which I almost didn't go to, and speaking to Libby Tucker, who I almost dodged.

It's normal to have limiting beliefs about ourselves. It's about what we do with those beliefs. The stories we tell ourselves manifest in our outer experience. We are able to actually change our lives by changing our stories.

I decided to accept whatever speaking gigs I was offered. The more I practiced, the easier it became, and public speaking transformed from being my biggest fear to becoming my sweet spot. I spoke publicly twenty-five times before first being paid for it. I spoke a few hundred times before writing this book.

According to Guy Kawasaki, entrepreneur, investor, and Chief Evangelist at Canva, we should practice an investor pitch at least twenty-five times before meeting with a venture capitalist. I suggest we apply that advice in telling our stories.

Before I speak, I rewrite my script several times, improving it with each iteration. I prefer to practice in front of a real audience, though I also record myself and use the mirror. If we can't empower ourselves with our own story, we can't empower others with it.

It's important to always start with our story. By taking people into the scene, we create tension and drama. If it's uncomfortable, chances are you're getting it right. Because it means the listeners are in suspense, waiting to hear what is going to happen next.

We Are Snapshots

"I tell myself I am a recovering awkward person. This is my PORTABLE PARABLE—a story I tell in a few words. The key to that story is the word 'RECOVERING.' When I have an awkward moment I remind myself of my story—I am still in recovery! And that gives me hope."

- Vanessa Van Edwards, Author of *Captivate* and Behavioral Investigator at Science of People

I often introduce myself on stage as a recovering perfectionist. It helps me connect on a deeper level with my audience and also takes the pressure off of delivering a perfect talk.

How can we best describe ourselves when speaking in front of a room? It can't take too long or be confusing. Explaining ourselves in a paragraph, or positioning ourselves quickly and clearly can be difficult.

The **Snapshot Bio** is an excellent tool to help hybridpreneurs describe the different hats we wear.

SNAPSHOT BIO

SPEAKER

DESCRIPTION + IMPACT

AUTHOR

DESCRIPTION + IMPACT

RESEARCHER

DESCRIPTION + IMPACT

ADJUNCT PROFESSOR

DESCRIPTION + IMPACT

SOCIAL INNOVATOR

DESCRIPTION + IMPACT

ENTREPRENEUR

DESCRIPTION + IMPACT

As I shared in Chapter 3, I'm an entrepreneur, innovation strategist, author, speaker, researcher, adjunct professor, social innovator, foodie, traveler, and design thinker. And now instead of feeling embarrassed to be a generalist, I've learned to embrace it. I am, after all, a hybridpreneur, and the Snapshot Bio enables others to understand those different hats without being confused. Regardless of who I'm speaking to, I am Saleema Vellani, an adventurous, curious woman who loves food, dance, and travel. My story is unique. So is yours.

It's important to prioritize the hats and titles that are more strategic to where we want to end up, rather than where we've been. This often happens with HOW we present our stories rather than which stories we choose. For instance, instead of sharing my hydroponics and refugee stories from the context of being an international development practitioner, I often find it more strategic to position myself as an innovation strategist in those stories.

We can use the **Sweet Spot Mapping** tool from Chapter 3 to think about the stories that best express who we've evolved into and the direction we're heading. Which titles feel most authentic? What's our portable parable? How can we incorporate it as one of our titles?

It's How We Show Up

"Whether we like to admit it or not, we decide if we like someone, if we trust someone, and if we want a relationship with someone, within the first few seconds of meeting them."

- Vanessa Van Edwards

As I continued practicing my story, I began appreciating the need to establish trust and connect with my audience to deliver my message. I struggled to figure out what to do with my hands and body gestures when on a stage, or even when networking. I'd often hold a cup in one hand and my purse in the other so that I didn't feel awkward.

I discovered the famous work of Albert Mehrabian.[26] Mehrabian's study showed that up to ninety-three percent of our emotional communication is nonverbal.

While this study is often misquoted and misunderstood, the basic point is that words do not fully communicate our meaning, or even come close to it, especially in conveying our emotions, which is the main thing that creates connection and impact.

As Vanessa Van Edwards points out, famous silent characters prove it as well as or better than academic studies do. Charlie Chaplin, Silent Bob, Teller from Penn & Teller, Wall-E, Courage the Cowardly Dog—the list goes on of well-crafted characters who can portray the spectrum of emotion without uttering a syllable. We don't just tell our stories, we show them.

I got to know Van Edwards when I signed up for her online course on body language for entrepreneurs. Van Edwards, who calls herself a "recovering awkward person," is the Founder and Behavioral Investigator at Science of People. She helps people master non-verbal communication for both in-person and digital encounters. I asked her how we can become better storytellers. She responded:

"Emotion! We are turned on and get tuned in to emotion.That's both sharing stories that trigger emotion AND sharing our stories with emotion. The biggest mistake speakers make is that they over-rehearse their emotions right out of their talk. If you talk about a moment of awe, sound awesome. If you talk about a moment of pride, sound proud. If you talk about a moment of sadness, showcase the sadness. Highlight emotions for yourself and others. Professional communication has gotten more and more sterile. We need stories to stay awake and engaged. We need stories to keep us off autopilot. We need stories to stay connected in a more and more virtual world. Stories make people and connections feel real."

BODY LANGUAGE BREAKDOWN

FACE: Facial expressions are similar throughout the world. The seven universal micro-expressions include: disgust, anger, fear, sadness, happiness, surprise, and contempt.

HEAD: Your head movements reveal much more about your attitude than you think. The speed and frequency with which you nod, shake, and tilt can convey different meanings.

POSTURE: How you hold your body can convey a wealth of information about your emotions and personality characteristics, such as whether you're confident, open, or submissive.

HANDS: Your hands reveal your authority, your trustworthiness, and how you're feeling in the moment. What you do with your hands is critical when it comes to first impressions.

MOVEMENT: How you move, walk, stand, or sit tells others whether or not you care, if you're being truthful, and how well you're listening.

Learning about body language helped me transform the way I felt as well as the way I showed up. Before taking these body language courses, I never knew how to stand confidently, how to pace on a stage, or what to do with my hands when talking to someone. My storytelling improved, the quality of my networking increased, my confidence grew, and my ability to influence and impact skyrocketed.

As we have decreased our face-to-face interactions and exist in a more virtual world, we have a greater responsibility to convey our trustworthiness. Here is a non-verbal communication cheat sheet, the **Do's And Don'ts Of Body Language.**

DO'S AND DON'TS OF BODY LANGUAGE

DO	DON'T
✓ Get into peak state through power posing and mirror their body language.	X Power pose while in a meeting or room with others.
✓ Greet with a smile and a confident, strong handshake or virtual wave.	X Use nervous gestures such as fidgeting, drumming, or tapping.
✓ Flip your palms up toward the other person or audience.	X Cross your arms, clench your fists, rub your neck, or touch your face.
✓ Keep your shoulders back, your head slightly tilted, and use a slow, triple nod.	X Bobble your head, play with your hair, bite your lips, or fiddle with your watch.
✓ Wear colors that are aligned to your brand.	X Wear colors that will wash you out or clash with the background or stage.
✓ Read their micro-expressions and use their learning style.	X Plan your response while others are still speaking.
✓ Relax your eyes and upper body and be aware of your facial expressions.	X Use a deer-in-the-headlights face.

Living Our Story: Our Personal Value Proposition

"Having a voice is a gift that you and I often take for granted, sitting in America. Anyone can be a changemaker. Technology has made it easier for us to share stories."

- Nina Ansary, Iranian-American Women's Rights Advocate and Historian

As Ansary connects with girls and women in Iran, she often shares stories of young women who have shattered the glass ceiling, such as the teenage sisters who successfully launched Bye-Bye Plastic Bags, a youth movement promoting a world free of plastic bags led by two teenage girl founders in Bali.[27]

People constantly ask me: How do you know which story to tell to which audience? To decide, it helps to know these three things about them:

1. Context
2. Cultural background
3. Current challenges

When speaking to entrepreneurs, I share my journey as an entrepreneur. When speaking to students, I share more about my experience graduating into a crisis. When I'm speaking to companies, I share intrapreneurship stories and discuss themes such as inclusion, leadership, and innovation.

Storytelling can even be a powerful tool in mentorship, both for the mentor and the mentee. In fact, the role of storytelling in mentorship helped me realize how much story can still impact, even from a distance. One of my greatest mentors was the late Leila Janah, founder of Sama and LXMI. Janah built a movement around giving the poor in developing countries work instead of aid. I saw her in person twice during her book tour and followed her on social media.

As a fellow Indian-diaspora North American entrepreneur, there was no role model I resonated with more than Leila Janah—yet I never spoke to her directly. Okay, I made sure I was the first person to show up when I saw her in Lisbon and we exchanged smiles, and that was enough, because she told her story in a way that enabled me to be mentored by the story itself.

When the pandemic hit in 2020, business owners, aspiring entrepreneurs, and professionals seeking a career rebrand asked me to mentor them: "How did you build your platform and an engaged community? How did you start creating a name for yourself? How did you build a team and grow your business?"

No longer able to travel to facilitate workshops and deliver talks, I found that my story became more important than me. Still going through my own pivot, I was already being called to live Saleema 3.0—to help entrepreneurs succeed, and not by accident, not in passing, but aggressively and actively, by embracing a new WE notion of self.

Innovation starts with I—leveraging our real story in unique ways, making non-obvious combinations of what already exists. But it continues with WE. It was time to start creating the story of my future—actually, OUR future. There was not yet an actual Saleema 3.0, but she was coming soon, to a theater near us.

We have made it to the end of WE. Many of the tools we have seen until now in this book can help us tell our story. I often use **The Ripple Impact Framework** (from the Introduction). It's also helpful to revisit our **Snapshot Bio**, our **Sweet Spot Mapping** tool (Chapter 3), and our **Great Idea Checker** tool (Chapter 4). I've summarized this all, and highlighted it via the I - WE - WORLD Framework, in the **Story Toolkit** tool. Armed with all these resources, we are ready to move on to the book's final section, bringing our WE to the WORLD.

STORY TOOLKIT

STORY	MESSAGE	CALL TO ACTION
What helped me get to where I am?	Why is this important?	How can others apply my message?

STORY	MESSAGE	CALL TO ACTION
What's my impact on those around me?	Why is this important?	How can others apply my message?

STORY	MESSAGE	CALL TO ACTION
What's my impact on the world?	Why is this important?	How can others apply my message?

Key Takeaways:

The Ripple Impact Of Storytelling
By practicing authenticity in storytelling, we can innovate while having a ripple impact on who we're serving.

We Are Snapshots
When introducing ourselves to others, we don't need to wear only one of our hats—we can share who we are as a snapshot of our different hats.

It's How We Show Up
We can tell the most impactful stories by sharing them with emotion and triggering emotion while using nonverbal communication.

Living Our Story: Our Personal Value Proposition
Don't just tell our story, live it, starting with I, leveraging WE, and impacting the WORLD.

"WHEN FOUNDERS ARE WORKING TO TAKE THEIR COMPANY FROM growth to scale, THE VALUE OF CONNECTING WITH THE RIGHT MENTORS CAN'T BE UNDERESTIMATED."

- KEN WILSON, RESEARCHER + SOCIAL IMPACT INVESTOR

"AS YOU CENTER IN ON SHARING THE WORK YOU DO IN YOUR STORY, IT'S IMPORTANT TO CONSIDER THE CULTURAL CONTEXT OF WHO YOU'RE SPEAKING TO. HOW DO OTHERS FEEL WHEN YOU TELL YOUR STORY?"

- TORIAN RICHARDSON
GLOBAL DIVERSITY RECRUITING LEADER, NVIDIA

"STORY IS LIKE A COMPUTER PROGRAM THAT YOU LOAD INTO SOMEONE'S MIND SO THEY CAN PLAY IT USING THEIR OWN INPUT."

- ANNETTE SIMMONS
AUTHOR, THE STORY FACTOR

"DON'T TELL A STORY THAT ISN'T TRUE BECAUSE PEOPLE WILL SENSE IT. THE ENTREPRENEURS THAT WILL THRIVE ARE THOSE WHO TELL A TRUE STORY. BE BLUNT AND HONEST."

- PIETER SPINDER, AUTHOR, FROM FEAR TO FREEDOM

"PEOPLE DON'T TAKE ENOUGH OWNERSHIP OF THEIR OWN CAREER STORY. YOU ACTUALLY WRITE THAT NARRATIVE."

- ZAC GITTENS, BUSINESS STRATEGIST + STARTUP MENTOR

"WHEN YOU HAVE *an idea,* YOU DON'T HAVE TO WAIT UNTIL IT'S FULLY COOKED TO SPEAK ABOUT IT."

- *Lionel Bodin*
MANAGING DIRECTOR
ACCENTURE DEVELOPMENT PARTNERSHIPS

"IF YOU WANT TO INFLUENCE PEOPLE'S CHOICES, YOU WILL FIND THAT THE MOST POWERFUL FORM OF INFLUENCE IS ALWAYS PERSONAL."

- *Annette Simmons*
AUTHOR, THE STORY FACTOR

"THE BEST STORIES COME OUT OF PEOPLE WHO ARE LIVING THEIR OWN STORY AND DON'T LIMIT THEMSELVES TO THE STATUS QUO. THEY ARE OPEN TO CHANGING THE STORY AS THEY GO."

- SANGRAM VAJRE, AUTHOR + CO-FOUNDER, TERMINUS

"STORYTELLING IS SUCH AN IMPORTANT SKILL SET. EVERYONE SHOULD BE PRACTICING THAT RIGHT NOW."

- *Janet Roller*
HEAD OF BRAND, AUDIENCE + INSIGHTS, SHUTTERFLY

"YOU CAN BRING ABOUT CHANGE BY SHARING STORIES. TECHNOLOGY HAS ONLY MADE IT EASIER FOR US TO SHARE STORIES. I LOOK AT THE YOUNGER GENERATION FOR INSPIRATION AND SHARE STORIES OF GIRLS WHO HAVE SHATTERED THE GLASS CEILING."

- NINA ANSARY, WOMEN'S RIGHTS ADVOCATE + HISTORIAN

WORLD

You're now ready to move to the WORLD aspect of your reinvention journey. Hopefully you've learned how to express yourself more authentically and foster more meaningful connections.

In this section:

- You'll prioritize your impact by focusing on what's most important to your vision.
- You'll become intentional about growing an engaged team and community.
- You'll build a strong foundation to scale your impact into the WORLD.

WARNING: You may have new insights about the things we've already covered. It's okay. That's the point! Everything we've learned about I and WE takes on a new importance when we apply it to the WORLD.

ORDINARY PEOPLE SET GOALS
EXTRAORDINARY PEOPLE IMPLEMENT VISIONS

Chapter 9

Intentional Prioritization

Executing Your Vision

Did you enter panic mode when COVID-19 hit? I did. My pipeline of gigs emptied out. My calendar showed the problem graphically: from a crammed schedule of workshops, speaking engagements, and innovation projects, it was suddenly blank.

I decided that this was good. It helped me understand the plight of the many other hybridpreneurs who were trying to figure out how to adapt to the virtual world and run their businesses online. Did you face that problem?

Many friends and colleagues put their passions and dreams aside to be "pragmatic" and take on full-time jobs. Many asked me for advice. But I could see that advice alone—even this book—was not enough. What worked for me might not work for them. If I really wanted to make an impact, I was going to have to roll up my sleeves, get into the trenches, and deal with the practical realities of each and every case that came my way.

Catalina, my then-assistant, was more overworked than I was. And she pointed out to me something I should have seen myself. I had to make a choice. Was I going to focus on Saleema's personal career, or on empowering other hybrid-preneurs hands-on? I had to choose, and prioritize. I could not do both.

Our client Maya helped me decide. She was burnt out. She had shingles for the third time. Her hair was falling out. Her eyes looked like tiny stones at the bottom of black holes. Honestly, she looked like she'd slept on her face, except she hadn't slept.

Maya had just left a successful corporate career and was driven to launch and grow her consulting business. She was, in short, overwhelmed. Spending every waking minute on her business. Wearing all the hats. And not generating enough revenue to pay the basics.

I've seen this problem again and again—entrepreneurs managing their own marketing, client work, graphic design, website, and well, everything. Maya had a lot of drive but no direction. She was saying "yes" to everything. She had goals. Lots of goals. But she lacked vision.

Maya gave me insight into myself. I, too, had no clear vision for where I was going. I was happy to have reinvented myself personally and professionally, and to have gotten the book going. But if I wanted to help Maya, I needed clarity for my own vision. What was Saleema 3.0 supposed to be about?

For a long time I was told that helping entrepreneurs succeed is my passion and I should go after that. But I didn't know how, so I limited my vision to what I understood. Other people could see where I needed to go, but I simply couldn't.

What I COULD see was that my impact on the world would be seriously limited if I kept only looking after myself. Even just having Catalina alongside me made a huge difference. I asked her to interview colleagues on my behalf so I could understand my strengths. I figured they would be more honest with her than if I asked them.

From these interviews, Catalina put together a list of the things we excelled at that we could help others with: branding, graphic design, marketing, creative assets. The list shocked me, as I thought it would have been Design Thinking and innovation workshops.

Catalina surprised me again when she scolded me that it wasn't about what I alone was good at—it was about what we could do together. This insight gave me a breakthrough. It wasn't just my vision; it was OURS now. And as the vision became clearer, I started to understand where to aim our goals. It was time to start Ripple Impact.

Be Intentional About Your Vision

The future of work is being able to master juggling multiple hats—and all the hats need to align with your vision.

Goals help you achieve what you want in your future. Goals give you direction. Goals are great.

But I knew that at Ripple Impact, we wouldn't focus on goals. Because goals alone are dangerous, as Maya's story shows. We would focus on vision first.

By vision, I mean beginning from core values and beliefs. Goals help you achieve your vision only if your vision is clear. If your vision is not clear, goals make you feel like a hamster running on a wheel.

Vision is the powerful reason WHY you want to do something. Vision brings purpose to your actions. A vision needs specific, actionable goals, for sure. But it's the values behind the vision that make it powerful.

YOUR VISION = WHAT YOU BELIEVE IN + WHAT YOU WANT IN YOUR FUTURE

We all struggle at some point to understand exactly what we want. I created this **Vision Roadmap** to assist with that. It helps you clarify your purpose, vision, mission, and values so you can be intentional in making an impact. You can map it out on a piece of paper, whiteboard, virtual board, or anything that allows for easy access. Because our Vision Roadmap evolves over time, it's good to revisit it monthly.

Along with **Vision**, this tool includes **Purpose, Mission,** and **Values.**

Your **Purpose** is the reason behind your goal and vision—your "Why Statement"—which you figure out by asking yourself "why?" until you get to the authentic root of why your goal and vision matter to you.

Your **Mission** is how you plan on executing your vision, whether in the form of activities, products, programs, or services.

Your **Values** are the basic and fundamental beliefs that guide you as you align with your purpose, execute your vision, and fulfill your mission.

VISION ROADMAP

PURPOSE

What's your why?

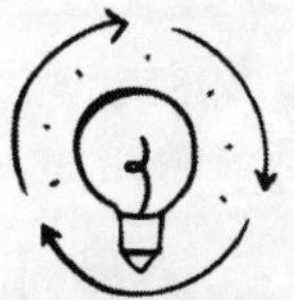

MISSION

How do you create that future?

VISION

What future do you want to help create?

VALUES

What beliefs and principles will guide your direction?

Everything that you do should be connected to your **Vision Statement**. When deciding if something is a priority, ask yourself: is this connected to my vision? How closely aligned is it? When you're not executing your vision, it can feel easy to blame your circumstances and come up with excuses. Taking full ownership starts by being connected to your basic direction, keeping your own agendas first, and living on your own terms. To do that, you have to know what your vision is.

MY NEW VISION STATEMENT FOR RIPPLE IMPACT: To help 10 million entrepreneurs succeed by 2030.

To make this vision statement a reality, I would have to execute along with our clients, not just provide advice. We would have to become their behind-the-scenes team. Teaching them how to build their own teams when they were struggling to keep their businesses afloat was pointless. We would help them grow their businesses and platforms first. Only after they reached a certain level of success would we help them grow their own teams.

Prioritize Your Impact

If you don't first have your own best interests in mind, then don't expect that someone else will.

Maya's strengths were as a visionary, but she was attempting to be a strategist, executor, and designer—one person wearing all the hats, pretending to be a team. She faced the typical chicken and egg issue: she needed to grow bigger in order to hire help, but not having help was keeping her from growing bigger.

Doing everything herself was burning her out. This took her away from the work she was passionate about and good at, the very reason she had started her business.

I knew those ropes. Again and again in the past I had wasted months on branding and logos, social media, and websites before acquiring customers. I had spent countless hours learning Photoshop, Illustrator, and PowerPoint. Then Canva arrived, a platform that democratizes graphic design, and all that knowledge was wasted unless I wanted to specialize as a graphic designer, which I sucked at. What makes a successful entrepreneur is happy customers, not Facebook likes. Cashflow fuels a team, and a team grows the business more.

Maya spent a lot of time talking about herself, her needs, her struggles. Yes, Innovation starts with I, but I don't mean like that. She was stuck thinking of herself as her business instead of leading her business. She was thinking of her own needs instead of the needs of her customers. This is a common conversation with early-stage entrepreneurs, who are in survival mode, just figuring out how to support themselves and become sustainable.

It's a terrible Catch-22, because when we're trying to build a business, the most important thing we must do is focus on helping others. Only then do you know what help you can most effectively offer—and you'll probably need to change all your branding and marketing after micro-niching.

We need to stop focusing on getting clients, and focus on creating outstanding customer experiences. We want our clients to come back again and refer new clients. This is another great reason for hybridpreneurship—to take the pressure of survival off, and allow us to grow our passion business organically.

Time is our most valuable asset, the only one we all share equally with Jeff Bezos and Bill Gates and Elon Musk. What we do right now impacts the next few years, and what we do in the next few years impacts the following decades. We have to prioritize our business goals and learn when to say "no."

Instead of just telling Maya these things, I needed to show her, and others. Catalina helped me put together some master-classes and online courses to help hybridpreneurs build their digital platforms and grow their businesses. I was surprised when hundreds of people would show up to these events—but Catalina wasn't. She also wasn't as excited as I was by the turnout, because it wasn't resulting in income or real impact.

She suggested we bring Sean, a business strategist, on board to turn my vision into a reality. The first thing Sean told me was to stop doing all those free online classes, as they didn't provide lasting value. Instead, he said, we should focus on helping a few key clients end-to-end. I started declining Zoom speaking engagements to spend my time creating sustainable learning content. I significantly reduced speaking to larger organizations to focus on helping hybridpreneurs. We added a marketing manager to help amplify our efforts. In short, we had to cut out a lot to get more done.

Fast forward ten years. Will you be able to say you spent your last decade wisely? Or are you just keeping busy doing fruit-less activities? The **Action Priority Matrix** is a tool you can use to figure out what to prioritize among your different projects and responsibilities. It helps focus your energy toward the least effort with the highest impact.

ACTION PRIORITY MATRIX

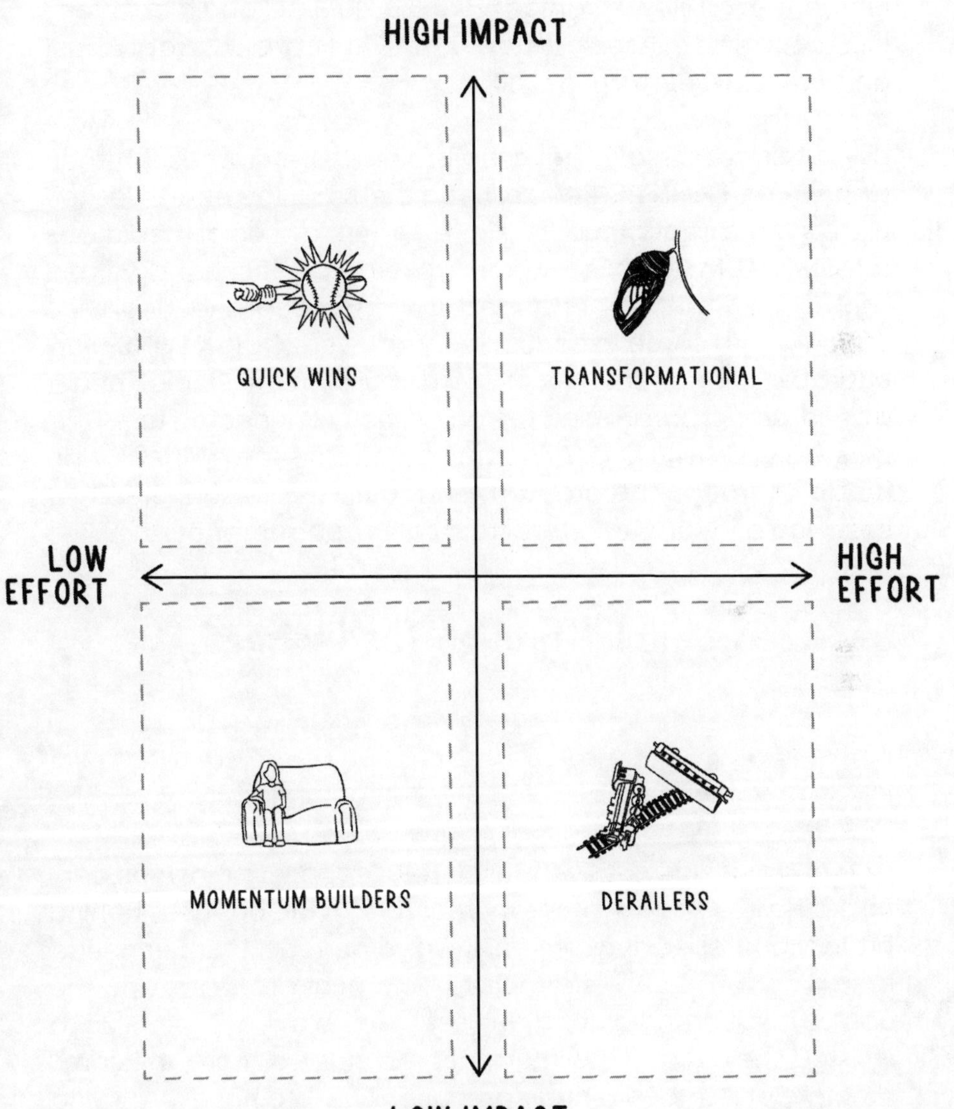

ADAPTED FROM THE ACTION PRIORITY MATRIX BY STEPHEN COVEY, AUTHOR OF THE 7 HABITS OF HIGHLY EFFECTIVE PEOPLE

Obviously you want to put your efforts into aiming for the **Quick Wins**—low effort, high impact—and outsource or avoid the **Derailers**—high effort, low impact. Low effort/low impact **Momentum Builders** can be worth some time, and high effort/high impact **Transformational** activities are probably best done with your team.

Using this tool, I saw that the virtual masterclasses, on their own, were **DERAILERS**. People loved them but the effort was too high and the impact too low. Engagement on social media was a **MOMENTUM BUILDER**—it didn't take much effort and helped keep our community engaged. Giving entrepreneurs advice coupled with some execution support were **QUICK WINS**—low effort, big impact. But best of all was building the Ripple Impact accelerator program and the community connected to it—this was truly **TRANSFORMATIONAL**, as each entrepreneur who made it through the program ended up with a success story that would in turn help transform other entrepreneurs.

Filter Through The Noise

Don't just listen to what people say.
Watch what they DO and observe their systems.

One of Maya's activities that she refused to let go of was participating in an online program that taught the business behind professional speaking. She felt it was a perfect fit for her needs, but I was skeptical. It seemed to be a pilot program, and the course instructor, Daniel, didn't seem to be a real expert. Maya insisted she needed the information and, even more, the community. But it added a huge amount of work to her overflowing plate, and what she was learning wasn't generating income. Worst of all, I felt like from what she shared with me, we could have given her better advice and help at Ripple.

The truth is that many of the participants got more out of it than Maya. But she was already so busy, most of the strategies didn't work very easily. She was getting grade B advice from someone who was teaching while they were learning it themselves.

Could she then recommend Daniel's program to others? No. Did Daniel even run it again? No, he didn't. I've seen this repeatedly with training programs. And I've realized that while the siren call of learning is tough to resist, it's critical to ask the right questions before strapping in for a whole lot of work that might not help us. We're getting sold products and ideas all the time, and it's important to be able to vet the advice we're offered before accepting it.

Is becoming your own publicist, designer, salesperson, or marketer aligned with your vision? Where does it lie on the Action Priority Matrix?

We're not just in the "Information Era;" we're in the "Too Much #$@& Era." People are selling everything. We're constantly inundated with information, much of it untrue. It's easy to click on a catchy Instagram ad that shows a successful influencer convincing users they can learn the secrets and strategies to win like the influencer did.

To find a gem of useful advice requires filtering through a lot of noise. Everything has a cost. Bad advice costs a lot more than we think. I used to think most people had my best interests at heart. The truth is, though, that even if someone honestly means well, it doesn't mean you should put yourself in their hands. Remember that old saying about the road to hell being paved with good intentions? That's a big problem these days.

You need to vet such programs carefully, do due diligence on the trainer and the graduates, interrogate the success stories, and investigate the competition. Most of all, if you want the best, top-notch advice for whatever your goal is, I suggest avoiding cookie cutter-type programs in favor of working with proven experts, even if it's more expensive. If time is money, the cost of bad advice and potentially the damage control is usually worse or by then it's too late—especially if it takes up a lot of your time. You may find you are unaware of what good advice looks like until you invest in it and experience the results from it.

It's made harder by the fact that real experts often give you advice that feels uncomfortable, while you may—be honest—prefer input that feels good. When you refuse to hear the tough nuggets, it can prolong failure.

You have to balance the type of advice you're receiving with how important it is to your vision. Each bit of advice serves its purpose. I was getting too many different types of advice from different places and failing to make sense of it. I saw a lot of entrepreneurs making the same mistake based on unhelpful advice they didn't know what to do with.

The hardest part is figuring out how to vet the advice you get. You do background research, get exposed to freebies, and get high-level strategies from self-professed experts. You might be too skeptical about great input, and too quick to adopt pointers that don't suit you at all. With all the fake news and gleaming profiles these days, you have to go the extra mile to see how credible someone's input really is.

I created this **Vetting Advice Framework** to vet information and figure out how to deal with the advice, depending on the quality of it and where it originates.

VETTING ADVICE

GRADE A | SEASONED SAGES

Consultants, coaches, and proven experts with deep industry experience. They've been there and done it and can help others with their wisdom and connections.

Tip: Make sure they are not obsolete and that their knowledge is relevant to the current market.

GRADE B | LEARNING DOERS

Consultants and coaches that have experienced some level of success who learn as they work with clients. They share becoming-an-expert type of advice.

Tip: Success can be hit or miss since they are early or midway on a learning curve. Watch out for overmarketing. Know your success metrics and goals.

GRADE C | MENTORS

A boss or experienced colleague who you can trust for specific advice where they have experience. They can often share stories and insider information with you.

Tip: Even though they have your best interests in mind, be strategic with what you ask for to make sure it's relevant to their expertise and experience.

GRADE D | PEER TO PEER

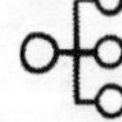

Communities where you're part of an inner circle for knowledge exchange and accountability. You can leverage the connections and referrals to potential experts.

Tip: Take your peers' advice with a grain of salt. What works for others may not work for you. Shop around when connecting with referrals.

GRADE E | NICHE NUGGETS

Books, webinars, online courses, and niche informational products. You get a narrow slice of what's shared, but miss out on detailed, tailored strategies.

Tip: Good entry point in your vetting process. You may pick up some great nuggets that catalyze deeper learning.

GRADE F | FREEBIES

Free information like online articles, Googleable information, forums, and reviews. It's useful to learn about what type of help you want, but increasingly less reliable.

Tip: Do your homework and extra due diligence. Use credible sources.

Maya was involved with many online courses and Facebook communities that weren't helping her. Worst of all, much of the advice she got in one place conflicted with advice she got somewhere else. No wonder she was confused and exhausted. She needed to focus on one source who was invested fully in understanding her unique skills and her blind spots. All she was getting were niche nuggets scattered around like bread-crumbs—no clear path, just chaos.

I had made the same mistake Maya did. I had hired short-term interns, fellows, and freelancers to help on specific tasks. Sean—the business strategist—saw me getting overwhelmed dealing with temporary talent, and said to focus instead on hiring team members that were in it for the long run. We needed people who were fully invested in the Ripple Impact vision, he pointed out. We needed 1 + 1 = 5, not 1 + 1 = 1.

Figure out how important external advice is by determining how aligned your goal is to your vision statement. Let's say you're wanting to learn more about how to get media exposure for your soon-to-be-published book, as I was. You may want to attend a webinar about publishing. You may decide to ask mentors for connections and join a Facebook community. You might have to hire help.

When seeking help, it's best to shop around, get opinions, and understand where your prospects fit into the framework before making your decision. For instance, a Learning Doer such as a public relations consultant with three years of experience might cost you more than you think, because they need more time to get the job done, or they have higher costs since they need a network of partners to help them. Even if they cost less money, they may not deliver results, as they may not know the best strategy for your specific case due to lack of experience.

Let Go: From 100% To 70%

Perfect is the enemy of done.

Remember, I'm a recovering perfectionist. That means, still in recovery. Like any addict, I need to remind myself sometimes that I will never completely recover. I was raised as a perfectionist, and it's in my blood. My family's expectations of me were high when I was growing up. If I got a grade of 99, I should have gotten 100. If I got an A, why not an A+?

When the perfectionist bug kicks in, it stops me from being productive and making an impact. When perfectionism rules our lives, we don't see our projects as a learning or growth opportunity. Instead, we focus only on outcomes and controlling them.

Are you a perfectionist? If so, where does it come from?

Mine comes from being a People Pleaser. I care a lot about what others think of me and am scared of being judged—although the real person judging me is myself. They say people are too busy worrying about being judged by others to actually judge us, but it doesn't feel like that, does it?

Half-hearted efforts have always irked me, whether mine or someone else's. I'm the type that would read an email several times before sending it and then re-read it again later to catch all the errors and things that could be said better. I've learned that the costs of all this tweaking outweigh the benefits. The migraines, the extra time and energy, the impact on the rest of my productivity: they're never worth the tiny improvements.

I've had to learn how to relinquish control and accept that others might have better ideas than I do. It hasn't been easy.

Like most entrepreneurs, I've had to go through the failures of making mistakes others cautioned me about.

What I have learned along the way, though, is it's better to invest too much in your vision than not to invest enough. This is your life's work, and the longer you take to invest in yourself, the longer it will take to get there. By trying to save money, I ended up losing a lot more money many times.

One example: I dragged my feet on creating a Global Changemakers Summit. It was originally supposed to happen in 2019, but I tried to do it using free labor and my own "free time" and postponed it to May 2020. Obviously it didn't happen, and now we will have to wait until COVID protocols allow it.

We cannot work at 100 percent capacity all the time. Probably not even half that. We're human. We get tired, burnt out, upset, and even unmotivated. And that's normal. It's all right. Sometimes trying to make things perfect is what stops us from nearing "perfection."

Technology helps us when we use it wisely, but we're not superhumans. At least not yet. Instead of aiming for perfection, we do better to figure out the areas where we can let go to get more done. Sometimes seventy percent is better than 100. Sometimes smart failure is better than dumb success.

After using the Action Priority Matrix to figure out what to do, you can determine how to manage your priorities using the **4 D's of Time Management** tool (Do, Delay, Delegate, or Dump) that I adapted from The Eisenhower Matrix. It's fantastic for when you're overwhelmed.

THE 4 D's OF TIME MANAGEMENT

	URGENT	NOT URGENT
IMPORTANT	 **DO** Focus on these tasks first.	 **DELAY** Schedule a future time to get it done.
NOT IMPORTANT	 **DELEGATE** Find someone else who can get it done..	 **DUMP** Remove from your to-do list.

ADAPTED FROM THE EISENHOWER MATRIX BY DWIGHT DAVID EISENHOWER

Here's the breakdown:

DO: Tasks that require your personal attention and expertise that are urgent and important for your business goals. Action these.

DELEGATE: Tasks that do not require your personal attention and expertise and are not a good use of your time. Pass these on to others who can do them better and faster than you.

DELAY: Tasks where priorities or deadlines have changed and that aren't urgent. Park these for later.

DUMP: Tasks or processes that are no longer important or required and would be a waste of your time. Remove these from your to-do list.

For example, if you're spending thirty percent of your time on social media marketing and feeling drained by it since it's not your forte, you may go farther faster toward your actual vision by investing in help while you take on another contract or more clients to pay for it.

Figuring out how to prioritize according to the 4 D's can be tricky if you've never used the framework. Tim Ferriss has some great advice to help you figure out what to do when prioritizing.[28] He suggests asking yourself three questions in this order:

1. **Which one of your tasks will optimize for skills and relationships that will persist past failure, and will lead to your bigger success, even if you go through multiple small failures?**
2. **Which one of your tasks will make the rest of your tasks easier or irrelevant?**
3. **Which task are you thinking about when you wake up or go to bed at night? Which one gets you excited, where you can have fun doing it and be yourself?**

I needed to spend my time on my greatest gifts: giving our clients feedback, creating content, tools, and resources, and running strategy sessions. I knew these elements, lived them, breathed them. I had to learn to delegate in areas where I was weaker.

Inspired by my own re-focus, Maya did the math and decided to work with us. It was much cheaper than hiring employees, training and managing them, hiring coaches that didn't help with execution, or hiring people to help her execute without a coherent strategy.

When she allowed us to help her focus and became open to testing with one team instead of with dozens, her business took off, and she was able to multiply her revenue tenfold within two months. It was only by focusing on listening to the "Seasoned Sage" (no, not me, my business partner) that this became possible.

Key Takeaways:

Be Intentional About Your Vision
Write down and visit your goals regularly, and more importantly, focus on implementing your vision.

Prioritize Your Impact
Prioritize your impact by building something transformational while leveraging your quick wins.

Filter Through The Noise
Do your due diligence and vet the type of advice you want to receive based on how important it is to achieving your vision.

Let Go: From 100% To 70%
Don't let perfectionism get in the way of your vision. Figure out what you need to do, delegate, delay, or dump, based on your business goals.

"There's no shortage of information. The challenge is being able to filter where we derive *knowledge* and be *wise* in **different situations.**"
- Ali Shakil, Associate Partner, IBM

"Investing is an **important tool** for **every single one of us** – individuals and institutions. It gives us a way to align your **values with our gains**, tap into the largest pool of capital on the planet, and start to shift a centuries-old financial system. Impact investing is a way to do this with the ultimate intentionality – **where is every dollar going, and for what?"**
- *Rehana Nathoo*
Founder + CEO, Spectrum Impact

"We can't get back time. Where are you in your life, work, growing your capabilities and expertise? How can you leverage what you've accomplished and learned while you're still growing? Pivot points are for everyone."
– Isaac Sacolick, Author + Innovator

"If you want to be *strategic* and get ahead, it's important to realize early on that time is your biggest asset that you need to use wisely. You can earn and lose money, you can go in and out of roles, but the one thing you can't get back is time."
- Adam Smiley Poswolsky, Generational Workforce Speaker + Author

"Don't prioritize easy. *prioritize progress:* things that actually move the needle, things that have meaning."
- Brendon Burchard, Author + High Performance Coach

"We shouldn't be seduced by the lone entrepreneurship flash of brilliance. Start by talking to your **friends** and finding groups that are passionate about what you're **passionate** about. Don't fall victim to lonewolf mentality."
- Ben Atkinson, Innovation Engineer, Toyota

"Chase the vision, not the money. The money will end up following you."
- Tony Hsieh, Former CEO, Zappo's

"Entrepreneurship is a team effort *where you delegate to others to accelerate your idea."*
- Steven Rodriguez, Ecosystem Builder + Regional Manager, Techstars

FACE IT TILL YOU MAKE IT

Chapter 10

Iterative Adaptability

Succeeding Through Failure

We stared at the screen in panic. The numbers weren't moving at all. The first two days of the crowdfunding campaign for *Innovation Starts With I* had gone well, raising one-fourth of our goal, but we knew that would happen; that was family and friends. The public wasn't taking this viral, and the whole idea seemed foolish now. This was the first public effort by Ripple Impact, and if we couldn't make it work for my own book, how could we make it work for someone else's?

I started to think I should have listened to my friend who told me I was crazy to launch a crowdfunding campaign in the middle of a once-in-a-lifetime pandemic.

"People are losing their jobs and their businesses," she said. "You're great, but you're not Tony Robbins. No one has money to throw away on other people's dreams right now."

She wasn't the only one. Most of my friends urged me to be realistic. People were inundated with needs and demands. People were Zoomed out. The night before the campaign launch, we lowered the goal from $25,000 to $10,000. The morning of the launch, we changed it back, feeling gutsy but terrified. It felt like a Rejection Ritual, except every day felt like the whole hundred days of rejection.

We got lots of "Congratulations!" messages. Not to be ungrateful, but we needed money, not likes. We wondered if we should have skipped straight to the second paragraph, with the request for a contribution or pre-order, and skipped the formalities. We had to adapt, and fast.

As it turned out, we had to adapt a whole bunch of times. You're reading this book, so you know how this story ends. But the road to get there was not as smooth as it looks now in retrospect.

Scale Down To Power Up

"Emotional resilience, the ability to not quit, is probably the most important (and often overlooked) thing in entrepreneurship—more than brilliance or talent or raising a lot of money."

- Leila Janah, Founder of Sama and LXMI

I cast my mind back to the memory of one of my first great near-failures, after I'd just graduated from college during the last great global financial crisis. After months of searching, I gave up trying to find a job. My best friend suggested that as long as I had nothing else to do, I should go abroad and get international experience.

I found a volunteer gig in Brazil, working with kids at a rural orphanage. It sounded easy and worthwhile, doing meaningful work in the tropics. But a couple of weeks before I left for Brazil, my soon-to-be boss told me that I would instead be helping launch a language school whose proceeds would fund the orphanage.

They told me we'd be staying in Ipanema, a famous posh neighborhood blocks from the beach. What they didn't tell us—or know themselves—was that our building was full of squatters, and the owner kept turning off the water to push the squatters out. It was hot, and not having water most days was not so nice. I wasn't very experienced in travel then, and as a Canadian, not used to dealing with such inconveniences.

I also discovered that the Portuguese I'd studied to prepare for the trip was useless. I couldn't understand a word. Trying Portuñol—Spanish spoken with a nasal accent—didn't help. I had to set up a language school while unable to speak the local language. Then my coworker, who actually spoke Portuguese, got a job and quit the project.

More volunteers arrived from the orphanage to help. We slept on bunk beds in the living room. The water situation got worse. We had to fill up garbage bins with water from the store in the neighboring building and carry them up four flights of stairs. Then the store got tired of us too. I started showering with bottled water, which I couldn't really afford since I wasn't being paid anything.

Still, the language school grew. I stayed late at the office to use the dial-up internet and washed at fancy hotels on the beachfront. I often slept at 4 AM after setting up class schedules on spreadsheets and had to be up again before 7. The only paid staff were the outsourced Portuguese teachers. As foreigners, we offered to teach all the languages we knew. Many of the volunteers were just looking for free lodging and often went to the beach during work. All the students had different demands for style, intensity, and even languages. Many of our group classes were turning into private classes at the cost of group classes. It was becoming unsustainable. Our business model was failing.

In short, it was not a holiday. I was in paradise, but to say it was uncomfortable for the young me is an understatement. Even then, inexperienced as I was, I knew we had to pivot. I didn't know the word, but I knew we had to do something.

When launching a new product or business, it's important to be agile and iterate: diverge, explore, and test different strategies and audiences. At the same time, you have to stay aligned with the vision.

I sent the volunteers to roam the streets with flyers. That didn't work. Everyone wanted to quit. But the head of the project kept urging us to try a little longer.

The problem wasn't just enrolling students. We had to rethink our customer experience and strive to build a community who would spread the word and become our champions. Our foreign students were fascinated that the proceeds of their tuition were going toward the orphanage, while our Brazilian students weren't as intrigued by that mission. So we realized we had to focus on the foreigners, and figure out how to get them to be ecstatic and write great reviews about us.

I didn't have the **Sweet Spot Mapping** tool then. But clearly, our sweet spot was teaching Portuguese to foreign students. So we stopped teaching French, German, Spanish, Dutch, and all the other languages. We were afraid of letting go of potential business, but it turned out to be the right decision.

APPLYING SWEET SPOT MAPPING

EXCELLED AT

We attracted foreign students who wanted to study Portuguese.

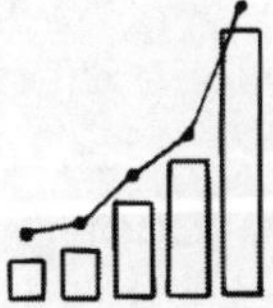

PRAISED FOR

The foreign students were passionate about our mission and enjoyed visiting the orphanage.

LOVED DOING

We loved building a community and arranging extra-curricular activities for the students.

OPEN TO TESTING

We wanted to test scaling up our Portuguese classes, creating a homestay program, and becoming accredited.

As soon as we focused on Portuguese and carved out our niche, the school scaled up and we could barely manage the demand. The lesson here was that the only way we could have known this would work was by trying and failing to do it the way we started.

It's not like we had invented the teaching of Portuguese, the enticement of donating to an orphanage, or the customer base of foreigners passionate about social impact. Putting these all together in a unique win-win way was the trick. No other language school in Rio, or Brazil, or possibly all of Latin America, had such a creative model of social innovation.

The new success happened incredibly fast, but we didn't live happily ever after. Implementing an innovative idea attracts competitors quickly. We had to reinvent ourselves again and again, proactively. We had to re-expand beyond Portuguese. How could we be better, faster, and cheaper than the other options? We hired more experienced instructors, offered extra-curricular activities, set up academic accreditations, and created a host family homestay program. We listened to what our customers wanted and prioritized based on their demand.

Newton's First Law of Motion states that an object at rest will remain at rest if no force acts upon it. Likewise, a moving object will stay in motion. If we stay at rest in our comfort zone, we're more likely to be stuck there, or forced to react to external forces. If we take action, we'll stay in motion.

In the pandemic, we've witnessed alert businesses transform and disrupt, and comfortable businesses fail. It's appropriate that this story is about a school, because the lesson for me is that we have to keep learning. Studying what a competitor is offering can help us better position ourselves.

The language school is today, nearly fifteen years later, one of the top-rated Portuguese schools in Brazil.[29] It became a for-profit social enterprise with full-time paid staff. The orphanage closed, and the school now supports underprivileged children in neighboring favelas.

Managing the launch of the language school started my work life powerfully by teaching me that I had to develop and maintain the resilience to reinvent myself if I wanted to become an entrepreneur.

Shortly after I left Brazil, I moved to Italy, which I shared about earlier. There was still a global economic crisis, and I still couldn't find a job. The resilience I learned in Brazil helped me get through my failures as a chef, a tutor, an emcee, and an online translator—and eventually supported me to work with my partner on creating our six-figure business.

When scaling from WE to WORLD, often it's not about doing more, in terms of variety. More often, it's about doing less—iterating and focusing—while impacting more people.

Make Failure Your Mojo

You often need to fail and hit rock bottom
to come out strong on the other end.

Fear of failure can stop you from achieving your greatest successes and biggest breakthroughs, because failure is an opportunity for learning and growth. But to extract such takeaways, you need to analyze not only the failed outcome but also the failure itself.

3 TYPES OF FAILURE

BAD FAILURE

This type of failure could have been foreseen and avoided with the right advice. It's the worst kind of failure, and it usually happens when we don't have the right talent, attention to detail, or structure and systems in place. It also often happens when we don't prioritize and utilize our time wisely.

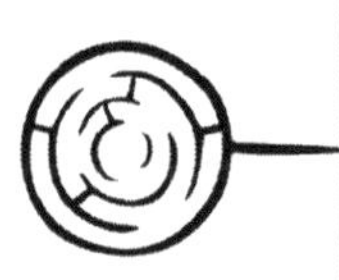

COMPLEX FAILURE

This type of failure is unavoidable and it's often hard to assign responsibility for. It happens when there's a specific combination of problems, people, and goals that have never occurred before. This type of failure is often experienced by fast-growing startups.

SMART FAILURE

This type of failure some of us need to go through in order to learn and excel in the future. It arises in situations when testing or experimentation is necessary. The project or startup might be one large pilot or in beta, or it could be a series of small failures that happen in iterations. This is often the type of failure that we hear tech entrepreneurs talk about when they encourage failing fast or failing forward.

Failure is a core part of entrepreneurship. It is important to be able to pick yourself up and find the right coping mechanisms. Failure is an opportunity to learn, correct, fine-tune, scale up, adjust roles, and much more. Today's failure is the key to tomorrow's success.

There are three main types of failure: **Bad Failure**, **Complex Failure**, and **Smart Failure**.

Bad Failure: If we had launched our crowdfunding campaign in March 2020, as we had planned to, it most likely would have been a **BAD FAILURE.** It was wise to wait a few months as people adapted to the virtual world.

Complex Failure: We launched our campaign with the uncertainty over whether people beyond my family and friends would support it. It was entirely new. We ran into all sorts of problems, especially ones that we couldn't control, like international transactions not clearing. It was hard to know whose fault this **COMPLEX FAILURE** was. Do we blame Indiegogo? Banks in other countries? Ourselves?

Smart Failure: We were actually aiming for **SMART FAILURE** as we started the campaign—knowing that it would take some time to get the outcome we wanted. The sooner we failed, learned, and iterated, the sooner we would be successful.

Make Your Business Model A Matter Of Survival

"Entrepreneurship is survival of the fittest.
Sometimes, the right decision is to stay the course.
Other times, it's to pivot or even close the doors.
One of the best exercises is to root yourself in the
voice of the customer. Write down five reasons from
the customer's point of view why you should stay the

course and five reasons why you should pivot or close."

- Doug Galen, Co-Founder and CEO of Rippleworks Foundation

Mark Horoszowski, Founder and CEO of MovingWorlds, told me that most people who jump into the world of entrepreneurship aren't ready for it. They are attracted to the idea without knowing the emotional resilience it takes. It's slower to learn lessons as an entrepreneur than at a job. Mark says: "You knew it would take long. It takes much longer."

In some ways, the best education you can get is experiencing what it's like to work within a fast-growing startup or in the corporate world. As an intrapreneur—which technically I was in Brazil—you have someone else's resources to fail with. When you're done, you walk away with skills, and experience, and you know what it's like to work with or lead a team.

Mike Duke, the CEO of Mortal.ai and former Chief Innovation Architect at Wells Fargo, advises not to develop a career for seniority but to build your own path. "Every course you take in college should be taken with your own business in mind." He predicts that nearly everyone starting high school this year will start their own company by age fifty.

"Entrepreneurs do what they can to survive in order to be patient enough to see the business model evolve. I pay my dues in order to make bets."

- Eric Koester, Professor of Innovation and Entrepreneurship at Georgetown University

Eric Koester started running his current business, Creator Institute, as a passion project while teaching and doing consulting work to pay the bills. He has found that eventually his unpaid passion projects turn into businesses as well. He feels we focus too much on creating entrepreneurs, when we should focus instead on creating project creators.

Keeping our focus on executing projects, he says, helps us develop self-awareness, build relationships, practice completion, and add value to our portfolio careers. It also helps us deal with failure better, since a failed project is a lot easier to cope with than a whole failed business.

Koester also talks about how business models are a matter of survival more than planning. By focusing on projects instead of businesses, he allows the correct business model to reveal itself.

Tradition puts so much focus on creating a business model up front. But Arianna Huffington's microsteps can apply here as well. Instead of a massive vision of a giant company, it can be far more successful to take each step along the way as a separate project. This allows small failures with far less risk. Fine-tuning and scaling your business model may come to you far more easily while you're already working on it, as opposed to while you're sitting and planning.

Remembering Koester's advice helped me reframe the challenge around the crowdfunding campaign. I was seeing it as key to the entire future of Ripple Impact. It wasn't. It wasn't even about the whole book. The crowdfunding itself was a project, and if it failed, I could use it to grow stronger with another effort. Accepting the possibility of failing freed me up to regain my resilience and continue toward success.

Still, this book is deeply personal, and having people not support it felt like personal rejection. I had to get over myself and pull in everything I had learned over the years about emotional resilience to keep my team inspired and get them adapting.

Face It Till You Make It

"System transformation relies on transformation of the individual contributor. If we don't change ourselves, then the systems around us won't change."

- Ellie Bahrmasel, Co-Founder and CEO of Further Faster Design

We tried a different message and audience each day. We added new perks. We set up partnerships with nonprofits to donate books to women entrepreneurs. We established à la carte sponsorships. I had to relinquish control and let the team get creative, and trust that we would eventually get it right.

We often hear the phrase "Fake it till you make it." I prefer to say "Face it till you make it," meaning just keep going until you get there. It's easy to blame your circumstances and make excuses. I used to blame-shift all the time until I was forced to become honest with myself. By building resilience and spending most of your time in your learning and growth zones, you become better able to navigate challenges. Resilience and adaptability are two of the core competencies Ripple Impact looks for when making new hires. Resilience enables growth.

You may not be primed for the highs and lows you face while running a company until you experience them. Regardless of the label you choose—entrepreneur, intrapreneur, hybridpreneur, leader—your innovative ideas will face resistance from many directions and even from within yourself. You need resilience to leverage your intuition, listen to feedback with empathy, and focus strategically, which we'll cover in the next chapter.

Once we iterated our strategy based on analyzing our audience's response, we got traction. We raised more than $50,000, twice the original goal and five times what almost had become the reduced target. We got sponsors and pre-orders from over fifty countries. By practicing "Face it till you make it," we were on a roll.

Key Takeaways:

Scale Down To Power Up
Keep your scope small and scale back when starting out, so you can fail fast in order to scale up.

Make Failure Your Mojo
Embrace failure—it's an opportunity for learning, growth, and innovation.

Make Your Business Model A Matter Of Survival
Start with a project where there's room to fail and pivot in the process before creating a whole business around your idea.

Face It Till You Make It
Don't take shortcuts and fake it. Build resilience and do the real work while adapting along the way.

"I SPEND TIME IN NATURE TO UNDERSTAND MY OWN SMALLNESS —**THAT HELPS ME PUT THINGS IN PERSPECTIVE.**- I ALSO THINK MEDITATION, PRAYER, OR SIMPLY REFLECTING ON **THE CORE VALUES THAT BROUGHT YOU INTO DOING THIS WORK IN THE FIRST PLACE** ARE ALL HELPFUL TACTICS IN MAKING IT THROUGH A ROUGH PATCH."
- **LEILA JANAH**, AUTHOR + SOCIAL ENTREPRENEUR

"**INNOVATION** IS JUST **REPEATED FAILURE** TILL YOU COME UP WITH **SOMETHING THAT WORKS.** NO ORGANIZATION EVER CREATED AN INNOVATION. **PEOPLE INNOVATE**, NOT COMPANIES." - **SETH GODIN**
AUTHOR + ENTREPRENEUR

"GIVE INDIVIDUALS THE SPACE TO FAIL. **WHEN PEOPLE KNOW THEY CAN FAIL, THEY'LL HAVE THE TIME AND SPACE TO THINK.**"
- **KIMBERLY COLETTI**
SENIOR DIRECTOR OF INNOVATION
SAVE THE CHILDREN

"**ENTREPRENEURSHIP ISN'T FOR EVERYONE.** IT CAN BE ROMANTICIZED TO SOME EXTENT. IT'S AN **AMAZING JOURNEY** BUT IT'S A LOT MORE CHALLENGING THAN WHAT IT SEEMS FROM THE OUTSIDE. **IT BUILDS YOU UP AS A PERSON.**"
- **AMEENA BUCHERI**, CEO + CO-FOUNDER, TELP

"**YOU HAVE TO BE COMFORTABLE WITH BEING UNCOMFORTABLE.** TWO YEARS OF THAT TURNS INTO YOU ACTUALLY ACCOMPLISHING WHAT YOU WANT TO DO."
- **KASANDRA MOULTRIE**, DIVERSITY, EQUITY + INCLUSION LEADER, GOOGLE

"WE HAVE TO DESIGN FOR **SAFE FAILURE**"
- BOB MOSHER
CHIEF LEARNING EVANGELIST, APPLY SYNERGIES

"THE *ability* TO FAIL AND HUMILIATE MYSELF ALL THE TIME IS MY GREATEST **SUPERPOWER.**"
-ALEX OSTERWALDER
CREATOR, BUSINESS MODEL CANVAS

"**An innovative mindset** is not learned in a training session, but rather through experience and courage to step out of our comfort zones"
- **Kamelia Hammachi**, BUSINESS DEVELOPMENT + PEDAGOGY SPECIALIST, KAIZEN ACADEMY ALGERIA

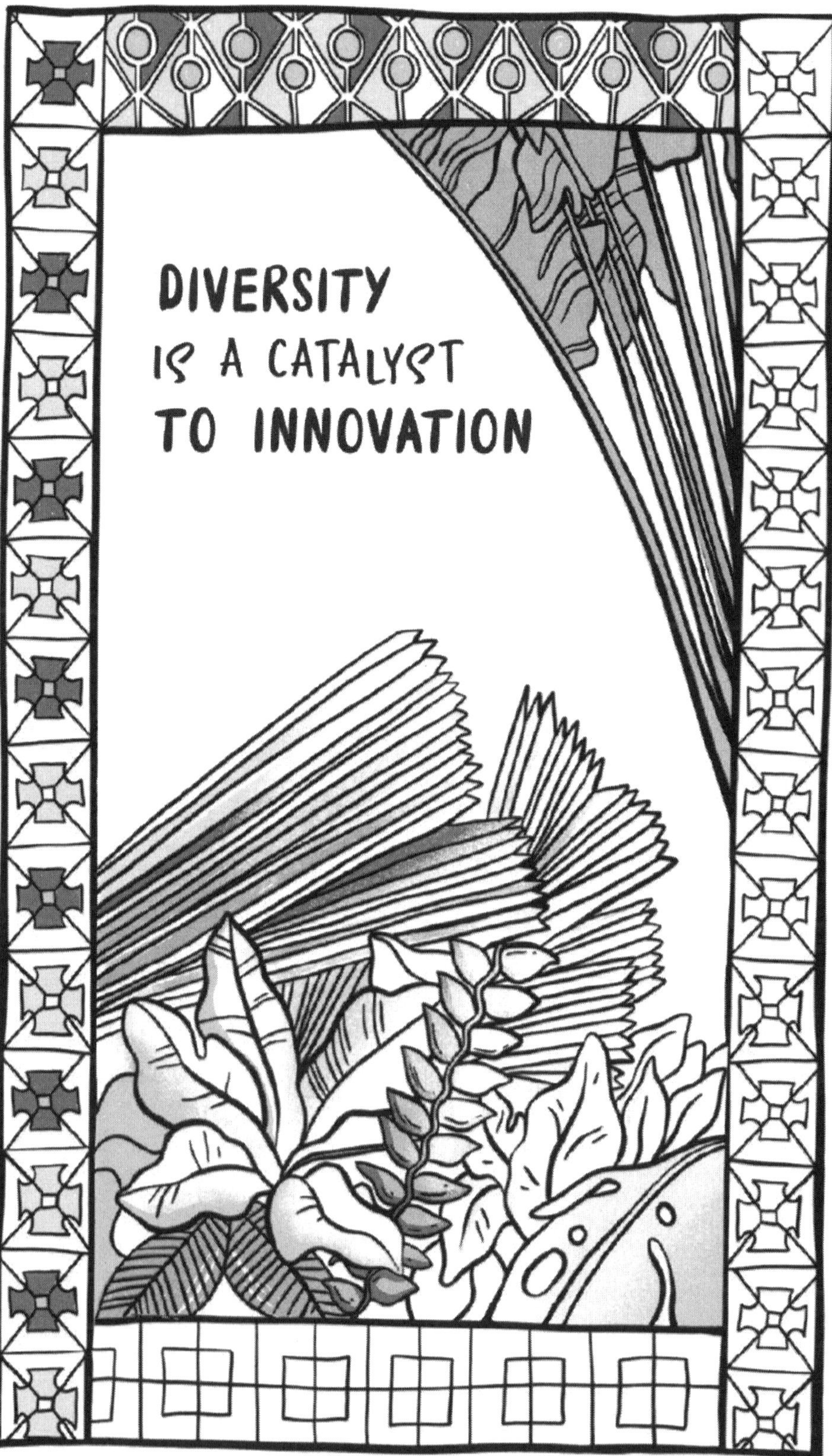
DIVERSITY
IS A CATALYST
TO INNOVATION

Chapter 11

Intercultural Intelligence

Adopting A Global Mindset

"How can I use Design Thinking to sell more fish?"

I couldn't see which woman said this at first. We were on Zoom, and a group of nearly two dozen Zambian entrepreneurs from Chawama were crowded in front of a single webcam. I had done Design Thinking workshops around the world in all kinds of challenging circumstances, but doing this one on Zoom, sitting in my own home due to the pandemic, seemed the hardest.

"I have to line up at 6 AM to use the community smoker for my fish business. I have to pay each time I use it and spend a lot of time waiting in line. So how can I sell more fish using your technique?"

Having traveled to more than seventy countries, I thought I had mastered intercultural skills—but I hadn't. I didn't know how to answer such a simple question. Because I wasn't where these people were, I literally couldn't meet them where they were. Through the computer, I failed at connecting interculturally. I found my years of experience traveling utterly useless. I wished I were there in person. Usually I do a lot of relationship building on the ground in a new country before delivering an engagement.

I couldn't give her the same advice I'd give a North American entrepreneur, right? I mean, in a way I could. She was dealing with the most common challenge entrepreneurs face worldwide: increasing profit. And yet, even though her problem was essentially the same as what I knew, I just couldn't find a way to get into her frame of reference so she could see the value of these universal tools.

I worry about the post-COVID world in this way. We surely won't travel as much as we did before, especially now that companies realize they can do the same online much cheaper. And can you really understand the cultures of different places without visiting them? How will misunderstanding those differences impact your effectiveness?

At the same time, the world is more interconnected. You are probably spending time connecting virtually with people you wouldn't otherwise have the opportunity to connect with—such as, in my case, the Zambian entrepreneurs.

The crowdfunding campaign for this book is what led me to these Zambian entrepreneurs. The Founder of Join The Journey—a nonprofit that provides microloans and business mentorship to resilient female entrepreneurs in hard-hit places—saw the book campaign on Twitter. He offered to help support the book launch in exchange for our support of the Zambian entrepreneurs. We announced the book several months later at their virtual fashion show. The online world enables new opportunities you wouldn't have even thought of beforehand.

But then, what good does it do if you lose the opportunity to understand the other cultures you're working with because you're just in and out on the way to the kitchen? How can you develop cultural awareness from halfway across the planet?

Develop Cultural Self-Awareness

"People are feeling less prone to identify with a specific country. Exploring different places to find what home means to us in the present moment enables us to open our minds and create a flourishing entrepreneurial lifestyle."

- Aiman Kabli, Futurist and Investor

Ironically, cultural awareness starts with self-awareness. While I was living in Italy, I didn't have friends, other than those I "inherited" from my partner. My days consisted of running the translation business. At night, my partner and I would go out with his friends for a "passeggiata"—an evening stroll on the pedestrian promenade for pizza or gelato. None of them spoke much English, so I was either the quiet observant one—or, if a joke was being translated for me, the sudden center of attention.

I wanted to get closer to them, to talk about my experiences living around the world and all the places on my bucket list. I wanted to learn about where they had traveled, but soon learned that most people in Reggio Calabria hadn't even been to Venice or Pisa. I always got awkward reactions and a change of subject.

My partner said, "You can't always talk about what interests you. You also have to talk about what would interest them."

That stuck with me. How could I have an interesting conversation with people I had so little in common with? As a perfectionist, I've always wanted to fix every problem instead of being willing to just accept them, and this often stopped me from building meaningful connections. I was lucky to have experienced the world, but not everyone has that privilege—nor that desire.

"The inward, transformative journey of cultural intelligence involves a heightened understanding of our own cultural background. How does our cultural background shape the way we think, see, and love? This kind of understanding about our own cultural background. . .plays a significant role."[30]

- David Livermore, President of the Cultural Intelligence Center

When I stopped trying so hard to fit in, I connected better. Understanding how my own culture differed from (and was similar to) the Italian culture helped me empathize with the people and listen more successfully.

It has been the same wherever I've worked in the world. In Latin America, I was trained to engage in small talk at business meetings. In parts of Northern and Western Europe, I had to learn to not take bluntness personally.

This **Preparing To Face Your Counterpart** framework helped me develop awareness in communicating and negotiating with different cultures. Erin Meyer, author of *The Culture Map* and an INSEAD professor, created this tool.

PREPARING TO FACE YOUR COUNTERPART

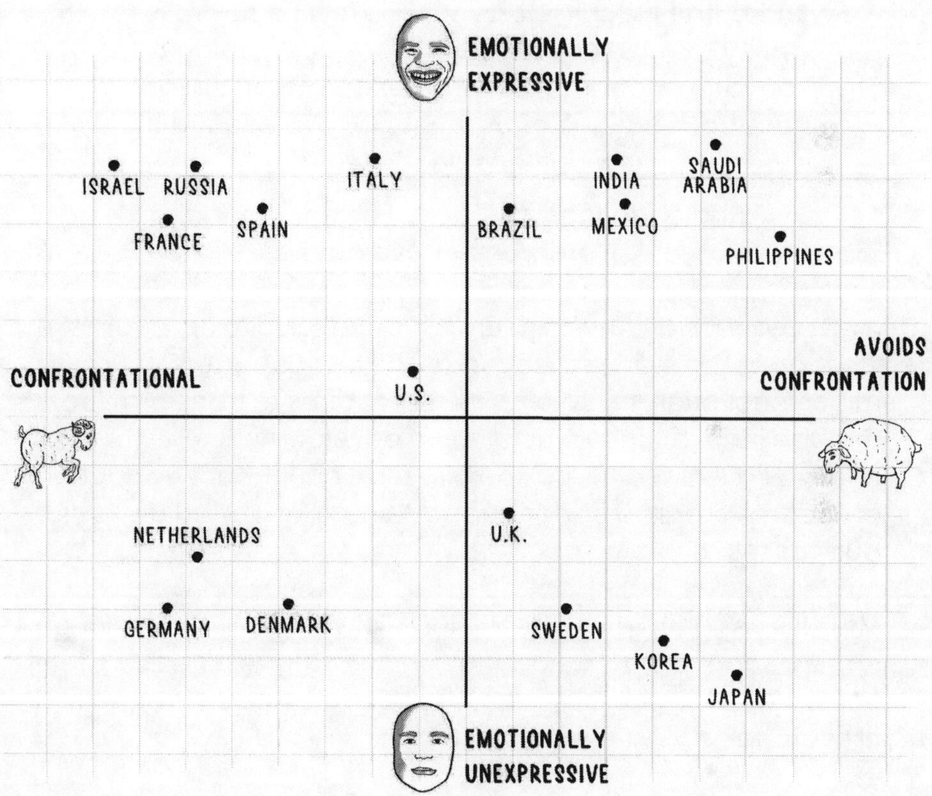

ADAPTED FROM PREPARING TO FACE YOUR COUNTERPART BY ERIN MEYER, AUTHOR AND PROFESSOR AT INSEAD BUSINESS SCHOOL.

By experiencing and studying other cultures, you'll get better at connecting across cultural boundaries and be more successful in doing business with them. More importantly, this increase in empathy will help you connect better with everyone else as well.

Leverage Languages And Divergent Thinking

"One of the most important skills for the future is the ability to have conversations about anything with anyone under any circumstances—to listen and share from a place of authenticity. We need to have a wider lens on the world."

- Shalonda Ingram, Social Entrepreneur and Community Developer

A few years before the pandemic hit, I traveled to Rio again. We were about to start a meeting at the headquarters of Brazil's major innovation institution, FINEP, that aims to transform Brazil through innovation for sustainable development. We were sitting with our research partners to plan our impact evaluation of federal programs that support small and medium-sized businesses.

My boss assigned me to be the interviewer. What? Even though I had become much more fluent in Portuguese, I didn't feel comfortable in the business vocabulary. I was sure I would mess it up.

It reminded me of when I'd been in the Dominican Republic in my third year of university on a study abroad program. My Spanish was stronger than that of most of my classmates. Then I got a summer job at a beach resort in Punta Cana, and found that my coworkers spoke several languages fluently—overnight I went from a rock star to a roadie.

These experiences taught me how important it is to speak multiple languages, and speak them as well as possible. When you can speak in another person's language, it removes so many barriers. My Spanish skills today have helped us open a second headquarters in Colombia for Ripple Impact, for instance.

Even just a few words or phrases can make a huge difference, taking you off the beaten path and into people's hearts and homes. It helps you learn a country's culture better. When I travel to a new country, I try to learn as much of the local language as I can before I go. Before I went to Egypt, I hired an Arabic teacher based in Cairo for virtual lessons. This came in handy again when I traveled to Morocco.

According to research,[31] learning a language changes the structure of your brain using neuroplasticity—regardless of how old you are. It also expands your creativity and innovation skills and enhances all four divergent thinking abilities: fluency, elaboration, originality, and flexibility. It builds memory and improves your ability to multitask, contributes to higher overall aptitude, and increases attention span.

Intercultural skills coupled with language skills add up to a global mindset. And yet, research shows that there is a serious foreign language skills gap in the workforce. Nine out of ten U.S. employers report that they rely on U.S.-based employees with language skills other than English. A majority of employers report that their need for foreign languages has increased over the past five years and project that it will continue to grow.[32]

Being able to communicate in more than one language helps you thrive in your work. Being multilingual immediately widens your market., Many of the most successful founders and CEOs are multilingual. Speaking multiple languages helps you to expand globally. Best of all, you can learn a language efficiently using the same online tools that can otherwise alienate you.

Mine The Global Talent Pool

"The benefits of tapping into a global remote talent pool outweigh hiring locally. More candidates inevitably means more high-quality candidates."

- Alari Aho, Co-Founder and CEO of Toggl Hire

Another way to use the virtual world to your intercultural benefit is by bringing together teams from diverse geographic locations. When I worked for Elance as a brand evangelist and storyteller, my job was to share the story of how I was able to grow businesses by leveraging talent on a global scale. But most people didn't listen to me. Instead, they shared stories of miserable experiences hiring contractors in other countries and blamed the contractors, as in: "I don't trust working with people in other countries."

But it's not about where the talent is. It's about how you manage the talent. In our new virtual world, you need to learn how to delegate and manage across cultures if you want to thrive. Leveraging the cost-effectiveness of the global talent pool can be a huge benefit to a company.

When I launched my online translation business, the market demand was not for my skill as a native English-speaking translator. What was needed was translation from English into other languages. It was often challenging to source great talent for less common languages such as Czech, Hungarian, Swedish, and Dutch, but for the more common ones, such as German, French, Italian, Spanish, and Portuguese, it was a breeze. We were able to enjoy a large profit margin by keeping overheads low.

As an international development professional who has lived in five countries, speaks five languages fluently, and has traveled to over seventy countries, working with people from different cultures comes naturally to me. I feel out of place in a homogeneous environment.

Forty-five percent of companies worldwide were impacted by a shortage of skilled talent in 2018.[33] These talent shortages will constrict growth for organizations and economies in the future of work if left unaddressed, according to Korn Ferry. Global labor shortages of 85.2 million skilled workers are projected by 2030, resulting in lost revenue opportunities of $8.452 trillion—the combined GDP of Germany and Japan. "The talent crunch—a skilled labor shortage—could ultimately shift the global balance of economic power by 2030."[34]

With the shift to working remotely, there has never been a better time to leverage the global talent pool to grow your business. Many countries have been adapting their visa and tax rules to take advantage of the remote working boom. Estonia and Barbados are examples of countries that launched visas for digital nomads to work remotely and legally in their countries.

We must move away from "I" and "similar to me" and embrace the diversity of cultures in building our teams, as it brings new perspectives and insights that are valuable not just from a business standpoint but also in making an impact.

When working with cultures you're less familiar with, refer to **The Culture Map Cheatsheet** below based on the eight scales in *The Culture Map* by Erin Meyer. It takes time and practice to get comfortable with what feels unfamiliar. As you connect with people from different cultural backgrounds, you might notice interesting patterns.

THE CULTURE MAP CHEATSHEET

COMMUNICATING

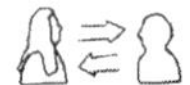

LOW-CONTEXT
Precise, simple and clear communication. Messages are expressed and understood at face value.

HIGH-CONTEXT
Sophisticated, nuanced, and layered. Messages are both spoken and read between the lines.

EVALUATING

DIRECT NEGATIVE FEEDBACK
Negative feedback is given bluntly and honestly without sugar coating, sometimes publicly.

INDIRECT NEGATIVE FEEDBACK
Negative feedback is given softly and diplomatically along with positive feedback, only privately.

PERSUADING

APPLICATION-FIRST (HOW)
People begin with a fact, statement, or opinion before adding concepts to back up or explain the conclusion.

PRINCIPLE-FIRST (WHY)
People first develop the theory or complex concept before presenting a fact, statement, or opinion.

LEADING

EGALITARIAN
Small distance between a boss and a subordinate. Organizational structures are flat.

HIERARCHICAL
Large distance between a boss and a subordinate. Status is important.

DECIDING

A B (C)

CONSENSUAL
Decisions are made in groups through unanimous agreement.

TOP-DOWN
Decisions are made by individuals, usually the boss.

TRUSTING

TASK-BASED
"You do good work consistently, you are reliable, I enjoy working with you, I trust you."

RELATIONSHIP-BASED
"I've seen who you are at a deep level, I've spent time with you, I know others who trust you, I trust you."

DISAGREEING

CONFRONTATIONAL
Disagreement and debate are positive for the team or organization.

AVOIDS CONFRONTATION
Disagreement and debate are negative for the team or organization.

SCHEDULING

LINEAR TIME
Project steps are approached sequentially, focused on meeting the deadline without interruptions.

FLEXIBLE TIME
Project steps are approached fluidly, changing tasks as opportunities arrive, allowing interruptions.

ADAPTED FROM THE CULTURE MAP BY ERIN MEYER

We should be aware of our assumptions and biases before dealing with people from other cultures. People are usually different than we expect. The best way to build rapport is to find commonalities and stay authentic.

Having intercultural skills sets us apart from the pack. This does not mean underpaying overseas workers. By offering more than they would earn domestically, you can create easy loyalty from those employees. You can then retain the best talent more easily.

Ask yourself: how can you leverage the WORLD to reach your business goals and make your impact?

Understand The Meaning Of Home

"I don't know what home is anymore. When you pick up, go, plant roots and do it again so many times, you lose that sense of 'home' and really just become where you are. I think in that way, you replace a longing for stability and rest, for simply being—engaging in your present by building a kaleidoscope of relationships around you."

- Adam Cole, Founder of Join The Journey

I spent much of my twenties traveling the world and living out of a suitcase while searching for "home." But soon after I started putting down the slightest roots, I'd run to the next country. My travels looked a lot like the rest of my life. While most of my friends were following a specific career track, I was all over the place, volunteering, interning, working jobs, consulting, doing gigs, co-founding ventures.

I couldn't manage to find a place that felt like "home" any more than I could find a career path. I thought of home as the physical place where my nuclear family lives. Since my nuclear family was dispersed after my mom's death, I thought I had to find a new home that included everything the old home would have had.

But everywhere I went, I saw as many cons as pros. Tropical paradises with lower costs of living had security issues. Other cities were wonderful but too cold. The most beautiful, natural locations had poor connectivity. Australia was too far from my family. Other places had bland food, or no salsa dancing. Often, there was a huge language barrier that would take years—and a commitment—to overcome. Or I couldn't get a visa or residency.

While moving from country to country helped me develop intercultural skills, it also felt alienating. I finally "settled down" in Washington, D.C., home to many international expats. Plus, it was an easy place to travel from. It's where I've now grown roots.

The pandemic helped shake that up. Travel halted and the city emptied itself. Many of my colleagues and friends returned to their countries of origin or decamped to the suburbs, or put their stuff in storage and became digital nomads.

I'm still open to living in other places. Part of me still craves the experience of moving to a new destination.

I've learned that "home" is a cultural concept with many meanings. According to American philosopher Michael Allen Fox, while many of us associate "home" with familiarity, permanence, and immutability, it is actually "a restless, shifting, somewhat elusive notion."

The word "home" in English is derived from the Old Norse "heima," which refers not only to a concrete place but also to a state of being and a set of emotional associations. During lockdown, many associated "home" with loneliness and isolation, whereas for others, home was a place of comfort and companionship.

I now realize that, for me, home is a sense of peace and happiness within myself. A physical "home" is only home for me when I have the option to leave it and return someday. If I had to stay forever, it would not feel like home.

What does "home" mean to you?

Embrace Cultural Diversity

"I love reading the Bhagavad Gita. I've spent a lot of time in India, and going back to that ancient wisdom that so brilliantly describes the transition that we need in our own lives is something that gives me a lot of strength, knowing that the answers to all the problems we're facing right now have existed for centuries—we just need to reconnect with them."

- Arianna Huffington, Founder and CEO of Thrive Global

A lot of the people I interviewed for *Innovation Starts With I* suggested I interview and spend time with entrepreneurs in other countries, especially in emerging markets, to expand my perspective. It made sense. I wanted this book to be valuable to leaders and entrepreneurs around the planet.

I already made an effort to visit local innovation hubs, collaborate with entrepreneurs, and incorporate Design Thinking workshops whenever I traveled. By teaching Design Thinking to social entrepreneurs in Liberia and Morocco, interviewing small business owners in Zambia and Panama, and running events for communities of changemakers in Canada and Portugal, I enhanced my cultural understanding.

The challenges experienced by entrepreneurs around the globe are actually very similar, even though the contexts can be vastly different. Creating a viable business model, acquiring customers, getting funding, and finding great industry-specific mentors are similar everywhere. Yet Africans hunger for knowledge and mentorship more than other places I've visited; they already experience strong community, while Europeans crave it.

If you don't have a knack for languages, there are other ways you can build rapport. Carry a few thank-you cards and some souvenirs from home to share at your meetings. It goes a long way in terms of being thoughtful, building connections, and creating memories. It makes you stand out and be remembered.

Diversity of all types is a major asset in the workforce. Including not just cultural complexity but also different perspectives, skills, ethnicities, races, and genders in a team helps company founders better understand their target audience. And therefore, innovate better.

I realized that for us to serve entrepreneurs globally, Ripple Impact had to be a global team. Because it's not just about understanding Design Thinking. It's also about understanding Zambian fish.

You surely have a different experience with diversity than I do. You might have never traveled to another country, or you might have lived in two dozen. You might be part of a subculture I've never heard of. You might be living in a distant village and been exposed to the broader world only through the internet. The point is that embracing diversity in multiple ways can only be a benefit to your business growth.

When the pandemic hit, we saw it as an opportunity to set up a satellite office in Colombia, where our creative agency is headquartered. We have since expanded our team with members in Europe, Asia, the Middle East, and Africa. Having a team dispersed all over the world also does make leading somewhat harder, as I soon discovered. Harder—but worth the challenge, as we'll see in the next and final chapter.

Key Takeaways:

Develop Cultural Self-Awareness
Cultural awareness begins with self-awareness—how you see yourself within other cultures and especially how others see you within their cultural lens.

Leverage Languages And Divergent Thinking
Put in a bit of extra effort when exposing yourself to new cultures by learning about the language—study a few words and phrases or take lessons—it'll help you see things differently.

Mine The Global Talent Pool
Hiring people who are different from you—especially from other cultures—leads to innovation.

Understand The Meaning Of Home
Check in with yourself regularly on what home means to you.

Embrace Cultural Diversity
A lot of the answers to problems you may be trying to solve may already exist in other cultures.

THERE HAS BEEN A LOT OF EMPHASIS ON IQ AND EQ. THE FUTURE WILL BE MORE CENTERED ON CQ—CULTURAL INTELLIGENCE—WHICH WE NEED TO INTEGRATE INTO OUR DAILY WAY OF DOING BUSINESS SO THAT WE CAN CREATE PRODUCTS FOR EVERYONE.
- SHERIKA EKPO, GLOBAL DIVERSITY + INCLUSION LEAD, GOOGLE

"EXPOSING YOURSELF TO AN EVER CHANGING PLACE AND SURROUNDINGS CONSTANTLY **STRETCHES YOUR MIND**. GOING INTO OTHER CULTURES AND SEEING HOW THEY SOLVE THEIR PROBLEMS OFFERS ALTERNATE SOLUTIONS TO WHAT PEOPLE NORMALLY SEE EVERYDAY."
- AIMAN KABLI, AUTHOR + ENTREPRENEUR

"*Entrepreneurship* IS **DIFFERENT** IN EMERGING MARKETS, WHERE THE PROBLEMS ARE BIGGER, THE GROWTH IS FASTER, AND THE OPPORTUNITIES ARE GREATER."
– DIEGO NORIEGA, AUTHOR + ENTREPRENEUR

"THE WORLD IS ONLY GOING TO BECOME MORE CONNECTED. WE NEED TO CARE ABOUT DIVERSE *values* AND PEOPLE."
- JANET ROLLER, HEAD OF BRAND, AUDIENCE + INSIGHTS, SHUTTERFLY

"CULTURAL MINDSETS AND BEHAVIORS AT COMPANIES AND AT TIMES AMONG WOMEN THEMSELVES ARE TWO OF THE BIGGEST CULPRITS IN PREVENTING WOMEN FROM ADVANCING."
- *Aisha Al-Kharusi, Global Business Leader*

"AS WE INSPIRE PEOPLE TO *think* ABOUT **ENTREPRENEURSHIP**, DON'T JUST THINK LOCALLY. IF YOU WANT TO GROW AT SCALE, THINK GLOBALLY."
- STEVEN RODRIGUEZ, ECOSYSTEM BUILDER + REGIONAL MANAGER, TECHSTARS

"DIVERSITY CONTRIBUTES TO THE ***success*** OF A COMPANY."
- CHRISTIAN LEITZ
HEAD OF CORPORATE RESPONSIBILITY, UBS.

"WE'RE IN AN **EXISTENTIAL CRISIS**, OPINIONS HAVE BECOME CHEAP. WE'RE MOVING TO A MUCH MORE SPIRITUAL WORLD WHERE PEOPLE ARE GOING BACK TO ANCIENT TRUTH AND PRAYER."
- *Reuben Abootorabi, Founder + CEO, The Austin Agency*

WE DON'T JUST NEED MORE THOUGHT LEADERS

WE NEED MORE ACTIVE LEADERS

Chapter 12

Innovative Leadership

Getting Back Into The Trenches

The pandemic wasn't going to end after a month. Did you know that? Somehow, I was shocked.

I faced the same challenges as many entrepreneurs faced in the early months of COVID. My trips, workshops, and speaking engagements around the world were all canceled, postponed, or moved online. I felt another lifequake coming on. And having just written most of a book about how to overcome a lifequake by being proactive, I didn't really relish the thought.

I had already become enamored with the idea of impacting the WORLD with my ideas and teaching. How could I best ensure this? I thought of going back to work at a job. I thought this was the worst time possible to launch Ripple Impact or this book. I thought and thought and thought and thought and thought.

Meanwhile, while I was entertaining myself by navel-gazing, my colleagues and past clients started asking for help. They wanted to know how I'd gained so much traction on LinkedIn;

how I became a successful professional speaker; how I started and sold businesses for a profit; how I got my TEDx talk.

I realized that just telling them my stories and answering their questions wasn't sufficient. Just teaching and mentoring on its own wasn't enough. These hybridpreneurs needed help executing and innovating, not just advice. They needed a team. It was obvious and I'd known it for a long time already. I wanted to help them but I didn't have time to do both my work and theirs. I needed to roll my sleeves up, yes. But I wasn't a team. I needed a team of my own to be able to provide others with one.

Ripple Impact needed to get moving. Now.

Roll Your Sleeves Up

Start your business where you can afford to fail while you prioritize making your customers wildly successful.

Aliza was planning her corporate exit. She showed me her Business Positioning Canvas. She wanted to build a mastermind program to help Design Thinkers and innovation experts become better workshop facilitators. I noticed it didn't include success stories.

I asked her about this and she went silent. She then admitted she hadn't helped anyone do this before but was great at it herself.

I understood her. I often had the same impulse. But I'd also learned the hard way that helping others do something is not the same as doing it yourself. We can't take shortcuts. We must grow our platform in collaboration with our customers. We can't business-plan it into reality. We have to grow it like a plant with each success. I know, I already told you I kill houseplants. But luckily I don't kill businesses.

I told Aliza to help ten people in her audience from start to finish to create success stories, while working with them one-on-one. And she did. It gave her room to fail forward and learn from her experience, while taking each client to the end. Along the way, her mastermind program designed itself.

You have to practice what you preach. You need to get into the trenches and help others in order to learn what help they need. By helping Aliza and others, Catalina and I had no choice but to grow Ripple Impact. We brought on a business strategist and a marketing manager. Building the team accelerated our accelerator.

Our early successes attracted more clients, so we created a Beta accelerator program. We filled it within a few days, simply through telling my story—no website, no advertising, no social media, no video. Just the facts.

We over-delivered on value while setting expectations low. We set ourselves the goal of failing smartly and focused on getting as much feedback as possible to improve the program while implementing it. That would allow us to scale it up. We created a transformative experience for our clients that transformed itself as it went along. On the way, we used this **Feedback Matrix** to help with the scale-up process.

FEEDBACK MATRIX

WHAT WORKED?	WHAT DIDN'T WORK?
✓ Participants enjoyed the innovative concept of having a behind-the-scenes team. ✓ Participants liked the alignment of the strategy, design, and execution support.	✗ The personalized roadmap changed significantly for every single participant during the program. ✗ The results depended not just on our advice, but also on the skills and execution abilities of each entrepreneur.
QUESTIONS?	**IDEAS?**
? How can we create an order of operations upfront? ? How can we continue to serve the accelerated entrepreneurs as well as meet the demand from other entrepreneurs?	Launch a membership-based program and community where we can help more entrepreneurs while they also learn and grow together. Scale up both our business accelerator and creative agency to help speakers, authors, coaches, and consultants.

Helping others at scale starts with helping a few people. It's one thing to be a content creator, thought leader, or coach, but it's another thing to actually help others do the same. To learn how to do it, we at Ripple Impact had to become **active leaders**, in the trenches, getting our hands dirty, rolling our sleeves up.

At the pace the world is evolving, what you mastered five years ago is no longer relevant now. Teaching your clients how to fish is no longer the best solution. Instead, you must use your mastery to fish for your clients, so they have a delicious feast ready for them to enjoy while they spend their precious time getting better at what they are already good at.

This innovative approach became the unique selling proposition of Ripple Impact. We fish for our clients so they can serve their clients better, and grow their impact more and more.

Build Your Platform Authentically

When you position yourself where you want to be, you'll attract opportunities that will not only align with the next version of yourself but will also accelerate that version.

As businesses were forced to adapt and go virtual in order to survive through 2020, building a name for oneself digitally became increasingly important. Expressing yourself authentically online and growing your exponential self became essential, especially as work and personal lives blended more than ever before.

The number of business applications filed in the U.S. increased by forty percent in October 2020 compared to the previous year.[35] While this was surely partly due to government support for small businesses, the fact is that more and more people started wearing multiple hats. Entrepreneurs took on full-time jobs to ensure security. Employers incorporated flexibility to attract the best talent. Employees finally had time to pursue passion projects or build side hustles. The age of the hybridpreneur arose!

Many of our hybridpreneurs prefer to hide behind their company brand. They think this is smarter, safer, and better practice. But their business comes because of their unique skills and background—their personal brand, not their company logo. They need to build a platform long before they think they need one.

I was hardly an old hand at all this, at this point. Only a couple of years had passed since my first "on stage" speaking engagement. For most of my career before that, I too was hiding. I used the name "sweetgyal_143" online until 2004, and "Selena" for a decade after that. I worried that putting myself out there would make people think I was shameless in self-promoting. I was scared to show up as Saleema 2.0, and lost years in the process.

The easiest way to help hybridpreneurs over this hump is to provide them with a team of their own. This can help them grow their platform faster, so they can serve better, monetize their uniqueness and talents, and ultimately grow their business by building their own teams. And as we excelled at providing this service, Ripple Impact grew its own impact.

You may underestimate the value of building a platform, thinking it's reserved for thought leaders or influencers who already have a big following. This is not true. Building an engaged platform strategically before you think you are ready to manage one can help you thrive more quickly as a hybridpreneur.

Building influence is essential to making the impact you're striving for. It, of course, directly creates that impact, and it also gives you the flexibility to own and price your worth and be selective in terms of the work you do, giving you more time to maximize your impact.

Create Your Dream Team

"All innovation comes from humanity. We might derive it from nature or animals, but it's the humans that connect the dots. Diversity of thought is critical. An idea with a team of less than three to four people wasn't worth listening to."

- Mike Duke, former Chief Innovation Architect at Wells Fargo and CEO of Mortal.ai

I still resisted my team telling me the truth. As Ripple Impact got going full speed, they told me I had to stop doing so much of my "own" work and focus on Ripple Impact's strengths—business development, brand repositioning, and marketing strategy. I missed my old sweet spots of being the keynote speaker and telling my own story, to be honest. But with the pandemic, the shift was necessary.

As we ran our Beta accelerator program, we realized that people needed killer graphic design, which was not my strength at all. As I had done with bringing in other translators to staff the translation agency, we brought more graphic designers on board. At the same time, we brought on more advisors to help with strategy and execution for our clients. The difference this time was it was "WE," not "I." It was, in fact, WORLD—we were a global team working with hybridpreneurs around the globe.

Working on an amazing team is like having good chemistry in dating. It feels organic, challenging, fulfilling, and leads to growth. Most importantly, it's fun. It's impossible to be a strong visionary, executor, strategist, and designer all at the same time. And even if it were possible, it would be lonely.

Big businesses are always concerned with hiring the right talent, thinking about goals and metrics, and evaluating results. They think about the right mixture of personalities the team needs. The hybridpreneur doesn't think about this very much, yet because the team is so much smaller, they actually need to think about it more.

One of the main reasons why our hydroponics research won an award was because of our team's chemistry. We were all doing what we were best at, what we were passionate about, and what was needed to achieve the project goal.

Mike Duke spent years trying to figure out the blend of personalities that best lead to innovation. After extensive research, Duke realized that when people were self-aware of their innovative personality and acted on it, while being around complementary personalities, teams became twice as effective. And when people understood where their gifts lay in the space of innovation, their lives at home also improved.

As I have said since the beginning of this book, innovation is deeply human. A team is just a collection of "I"s. You must start by asking yourself: What are you good at? What do you stink at? What could you become good at that is worth becoming good at?

You can refer to the **4 D's of Time Management** tool from Chapter 9 to figure out what makes sense for you to do as opposed to delegate, based on your business goals and bigger vision.

My conversations with Duke inspired me to build a framework of the roles, or personality types, needed to build an innovative team as an entrepreneur. Let's have a look.

THE INNOVATIVE TEAM RECIPE

"I have an idea! There must be an easier way to..."

Strength: Ideas

"Let's turn your idea into multiple products at different price tiers."

Strength: Solutions

"Tell me your vision and I'll get it done."

Strength: Products

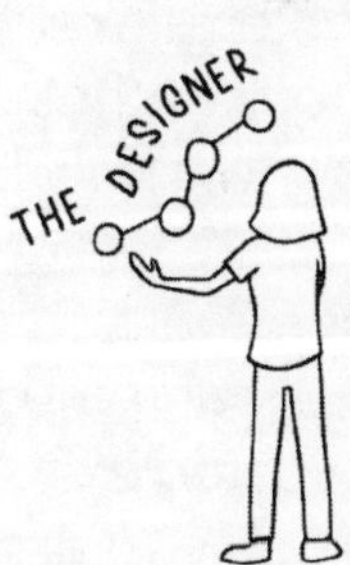

"What are your thoughts around this?"

Strength: Experiences

ADAPTED FROM INNOVATIVE PERSONALITIES
BY MIKE DUKE, CEO OF MORTAL.AI AND FORMER CHIEF INNOVATION ARCHITECT AT WELLS FARGO

The Visionary
As The Visionary, you are the big idea person, often questioning the status quo. You tend to be the face of the company or team and get the most credit. You are probably an idealist who tends to have an immense drive, including many passions and hobbies. When you master the skill of delegation, you are powerful.

The Strategist
As The Strategist, you provide direction to the Visionary. You divide the Visionary's vision into steps and components because of your need for and skill with structure. When you work closely with a Visionary, you can come up with structured products, packages, and services with lots of new features. You may like hiding behind the scenes and need someone to draw you out. You tend to be realistic and can even be a nay-sayer until you become inspired and see the answer to the problem.

The Executor
As The Executor, you are the person who brings the Visionary's idea to life. You tend to have a variety of skills, and you know how to leverage these skills and pull together existing resources to solve problems. Your own ideas may not always be the greatest, but you are enthusiastic to get behind the Visionary's ideas, and you know how to take ownership and get the job done.

The Designer
As The Designer, you create experiences for the team, the users, and the customers. You're empathetic, you communicate well, and you can visualize ideas from a variety of perspectives. You are tech-savvy, learn fast, and adapt fluidly to fast-changing situations. Strong in creative talent and thinking, you take the Visionary's idea and work with the Strategist and Executor to shape it into a valuable experience.

It's important to have a balance of these different personality types to create excellent team chemistry. You can work well with people you might not feel drawn to at first, and you don't have to always agree on things. What matters is that the blend of these diverse personalities enables innovation and impact.

You don't necessarily need to resonate with only one of those roles. You might identify with several of them yourself. You also don't need to have only one of each on your team. It is very rare for one person to play all these roles at the same time and do them well. Trying to do that is, as I've noted, a reason why many early-stage entrepreneurs fail. I have myself definitely been there and done that, thinking I could do it all. Even trying to be Visionary and Executor at the same time has never worked well for me. Knowing which role aligns with your personality and skills goes a long way, instead of taking on roles that don't bring out the best of you.

Which role(s) do you resonate with most? How can you ensure you focus on what you do best?

Design Your Own Ladder

You almost always need a team before
you think you're ready to have a team.

"Identify qualities in people that they haven't even seen in themselves. Test [their] different abilities. Look around and see how to prioritize their skills based on your needs. Inspire them to bring out of themselves qualities they didn't even know they had."

- Arianna Huffington

Honestly, we had no idea what we were doing when Ripple Impact started. I shared my vision and then instructed my team to be creative and build it, reassuring them that it was okay to fail first. I gave them free rein to experiment with different strategies. This freed me to focus on finishing this book and creating and testing different types of social content that they would then make visually appealing and amplify.

Within a few months, our online presence started growing significantly. I brought my team along on my journey from the early days, so they would feel invested in the vision and become part of it. My team helped accelerate my vision exponentially while I focused on what I was best at.

If you're like most entrepreneurs, you may think you need to be at a certain place before you hire a team. Maybe you've tried to juggle all the hats yourself, including the hats you don't wear well, the ones that drain you of your energy and creative juices and take away precious time from where you excel.

We talk about climbing the corporate ladder in a large organization, but these days the average American has ten to fifteen jobs throughout their career. So what ladder are they climbing exactly?

To thrive and pave your own path as a hybridpreneur, you have to create your own ladder. But instead of starting at the bottom and working up, you can start as the leader, at the top.

You are the CEO of your own life. Your ladder can be diagonal, more like a wobbly staircase. Your most valuable asset is your team—and you must work together with them, horizontally, towards the same mission. Defining that mission and keeping everyone on the ladder together is your job as the leader.

You may need to shift your perception of what it means to build a team. Building a team often overwhelms hybridpreneurs, and the anxiety prevents them from prioritizing this key step. A team isn't just the people you directly hire and manage. A team can consist of strategic partnerships, joint ventures, employees, contractors, collaborators, interns, fellows, mentors, advisors—any person or organization helping you achieve your vision.

When creating your own ladder, it's key to let your core team—the people involved in your day-to-day operations—lead and take ownership. Let them become experts. Create a culture where it's okay to fail and learn and let them be better than you at wearing certain hats—because they already are.

No one is self-made. You're constantly being influenced and influencing others. Solopreneurship is a facade. The most successful solopreneurs have teams even if they hide them. They may show up alone for engagements to better sell to other solopreneurs using creative advertising techniques and the illusion of doing it all alone. This leaves their customers feeling even more overwhelmed.

Whenever people refer to me as a solopreneur, I make it clear that I am not. I have a talented team behind me that specializes in the hats I don't wear well.

They also, increasingly, are skilling up to be able to step in on the areas I am good at on my behalf. For instance, on my virtual keynotes, team members engage with the audience to create a richer experience. We've even developed a "fire alarm" strategy that paid off when my building's alarm did go off during a webinar—they took over and handled the Q&A seamlessly. And no, this time my building wasn't actually burning down.

As a fast-paced startup, our roles are dynamic and we're always figuring out how to divide and conquer using the 4 D's. Having an organized project manager helps us get the job done. Every few months, we analyze what we're actually accomplishing versus what we feel we should be accomplishing, based on our strengths and weaknesses. We track all our wild ideas and discuss them monthly. We analyze how we need to upskill and what roles we need to hire for, using our **Team Empowerment Matrix** tool.

TEAM EMPOWERMENT MATRIX

TEAM MEMBER	WHAT YOU ACTUALLY DO	WHAT YOU EXCEL AT	WHAT YOU'RE NOT GOOD AT	WHAT YOU SHOULD DO	WHAT ROLES YOU NEED
VISIONARY	– – –	– – –	– – –	– – –	– – –
STRATEGIST	– – –	– – –	– – –	– – –	– – –
EXECUTOR	– – –	– – –	– – –	– – –	– – –
DESIGNER	– – –	– – –	– – –	– – –	– – –

It's important to keep our team with us long-term. Being part of our growth journey from the early stages, they not only feel fulfilled having been part of the whole arc, they also learn our audience and know how to engage with and serve them.

Catalina, who I started Ripple Impact with, has gone from starting as my assistant to becoming a brand strategist to now being our creative director, managing a whole team of graphic designers, video editors, web developers, and others. And she will likely grow to even greater heights as we progress as a team.

Arianna Huffington stresses the importance of giving employees work that is a priority, that's "needed and moving." She says that people working on non-essential work tend to feel dispirited.

"Inspiring leadership," she points out, "is about encouraging people to move into areas where they can have a bigger impact."

Move From Thought Leadership To Active Leadership

We don't just need more thought leaders.
We need more active leaders.

The bottom line is this: you must serve your clients. And the best way is to help them actively. The term "thought leader" has become overused and diluted. The days of being able to run a successful blog with written content alone are over.

This doesn't mean you can't be a thought leader. It means that you need to become an active leader first. Giving value to others in the trenches is how you can make a ripple impact.

Most online courses, business coaches, and group programs try to help hybridpreneurs with cookie-cutter methods designed to be cost-effective for the instructor, rather than effective for the client. They don't offer a strategy tailored to each person's unique vision and business goals, nor do they provide support on execution and creative work.

At the same time, it's important to build systems that go beyond the people and help your business run itself, by turning steps into templates or educational content and advice into courses and videos. As you build more case studies and success stories through deep-diving one-on-ones with your clients, you can identify the constants and variables and use the constants to roadmap your products, programs, and services in a more automated way.

As discussed in the last chapter, you have to figure out a workable balance between the cost and benefits of talent and advice. Of course, you always want to get the best results you can with the least input of your own time and money. But you have to start with what you can afford. This is why I so heartily recommend the hybridpreneur path, as it reduces pressure on your finances and provides a budget to invest in yourself.

Can you afford the training and turnover cost of interns? Does it make more sense to work with a contractor or a coach? What roles do you need long-term or in-house versus temporary or project-based? Are you building a movement? A company? A lifestyle?

The Ripple Impact Accelerator is unique in that while we do offer innovative advice on business, marketing, and branding strategies, we are also in the trenches with our clients, helping with execution hands-on. We help them grow their brands, expand their revenue streams, fill their talent gaps, and build their own teams. We have been there and done that—and now they are being there and doing that too. We are ripples, having a ripple impact.

The success stories of the entrepreneurs who made it through the accelerator helped us scale up the next version, and we continued to grow. From the two of us, we have become sixteen at the time of writing this paragraph a year later. And by the time you read it, we'll be much larger. We've had to start building systems that allow us to continue doing a great job while being approachable and making a bigger impact by reaching more entrepreneurs.

And thanks to my team, our systems, our clients, and our community, I am finally becoming Saleema 3.0.

Stay tuned for more.

Key Takeaways:

Roll Your Sleeves Up
Work hard to create success stories of how you help others by getting into the trenches with them.

Build Your Platform Authentically
When you build your platform and community authentically, your audience will crave your success and accelerate you towards achieving your vision.

Create Your Dream Team
Building a team with diverse personalities—especially a visionary, strategist, executor, and designer—leads to innovation.

Design Your Own Ladder
You don't need to climb the corporate ladder to be successful. You can create your own ladder.

Move From Thought Leadership To Active Leadership
Focus on becoming an active leader to maximize your influence and make a ripple impact.

"LEADERSHIP STARTS WITH RADICAL OWNERSHIP. ONCE WE ACCEPT THAT WE'RE HUMAN, WE CAN SEE WHERE WE CAN IMPROVE. WE NEED TO TAKE MORE OWNERSHIP OVER OUR LIVES AND THEN SCALE THAT OUT AT INCREDIBLE LEVELS."

- Zac Gittens, BUSINESS STRATEGIST + STARTUP MENTOR

"WE OFTEN THINK IT'S THE LEADER OR CIO THAT IS SANCTIONED TO COME UP WITH THE IDEAS AND THEY ARE THE ONLY ONES THAT CAN BE INNOVATIVE. WE ALL NEED TO UNLOCK OUR CREATIVITY."

-JEFFREY CARPENTER
VICE PRESIDENT OF INNOVATION, VANTAGE POINT

"THE MAGIC OF INFLUENCE IS LESS IN WHAT WE SAY AND MORE IN HOW WE SAY IT AND WHO WE ARE. INFLUENCE RESULTS FROM HOW OTHERS FEEL ABOUT YOU AND YOUR GOALS."

- ANNETTE SIMMONS
AUTHOR, THE STORY FACTOR

"INNOVATION is a team sport." - JANET ROLLER
HEAD OF BRAND, AUDIENCE + INSIGHTS, SHUTTERFLY

"THE MORE CONNECTED YOU ARE OUTSIDE YOUR BUBBLE, THE MORE YOU'RE ABLE TO INNOVATE—IT'S PART OF THE NETWORK EFFECT."

- ZAHRAA DAGHER
DESIGNER + STRATEGIST

"TO ACHIEVE SUCCESS IN INNOVATION, COMPANIES MUST INVEST IN MARKETING NEW PRODUCTS AND SERVICES AS MUCH AS THEY DO IN GENERATING THEM."

Jason Williams
MARKETING + INNOVATION STRATEGIST

"LEADERSHIP IS ABOUT IMPOSING YOUR WILL TO GET A GROUP OF PEOPLE TO DO SOMETHING TO MAKE PROGRESS AND MOVE FORWARD."

-STEVE DIFILIPO
CHIEF INFORMATION OFFICER

"A person's marketability IS A COMBINATION of who they are personally THEIR TALENTS and their ability to learn."

- ALLISON WRIGHT
ORGANIZATION EFFECTIVENESS LEADER, VERIZON

"IF YOU PUT THE RIGHT PEOPLE TOGETHER IN THE ROOM, YOU'LL ALMOST HAVE TO GET OUT OF THE WAY. THEY'LL WORK TOGETHER TO SOLVE THE PROBLEM GIVE THEM THE TIME TO UNDERSTAND THE PROBLEM, AND THE TOOLS TO SOLVE IT."

Jim Williams, GLOBAL LEARNING ADVISOR

"Influence is about energy. Someone who can inspire, energize, and get individuals behind them. Not just through words but through example, because what you do inspires them and motivates them to do better."

- COREY PONDER, FOUNDER, EM|PACT STRATEGIES

THE ONLY PERSON STOPPING YOU FROM **UNLEASHING YOUR IMPACT** IS YOU

Conclusion

Igniting Your Impact

"It's not a matter of the advice I gave.
It's a matter of what they followed."

- Simon Sinek

This applies as much to the advice we give ourselves as to the advice we give others.

Yes, Innovation starts with I. But as you've seen, it doesn't end there. We need to take it to WE and then WORLD to have a Ripple Impact.

I hope my own journey has shown you that the best way to change your outer experience is to do the inner work. Your inner world manifests in your outer world. We have the ability to change what we think and feel. And change starts with the mind.

To thrive in the Reinvention Revolution, we need to invest in being proactive, rather than sitting back waiting for things to come.

Everyone has their own journey. There is no right or wrong path. The trick is to become aware of when it's time to reinvent yourself, just like I did the day my building burned down. You can wait until you have a lifequake—or you can start now.

Use the **Ripple Impact Plan**, which I've included in this section, to help apply what you've learned in this book to your own life.

Whenever you're feeling the itch to innovate in your business or launch a new idea, you can refer to the tools and insights throughout this book. These tools have helped thousands of people that I've spoken to, worked with, or reached in some capacity.

By strengthening the **Twelve Future-Proof Capabilities** in yourself, you'll be better able to adapt to the uncertain, volatile world that we live in. I've summarized all twelve of them for you.

THE 12 FUTURE-PROOF CAPABILITIES

SELF-AWARENESS	You know who you are in your own lens as well as in the lens of others.
CURIOSITY	You go beyond the status quo and are open to insights and creative breakthroughs.
INTUITION	You act on what feels valuable to others without worrying if it seems strategic.
ORIGINALITY	You combine existing ideas in non-obvious ways that create value.

WE

COLLABORATION	You give value to others without expecting to get any back.
EMPATHY	You make others feel heard by walking in their boots and feeling what they feel.
AUTHENTICITY	You share the different aspects of yourself in a tactful way that people are receptive to.
STORYTELLING	You design your story based on where you want to go, not where you are.

WORLD

PRIORITIZATION	You juggle different hats while prioritizing your vision.
ADAPTABILITY	You learn from failure and iterate until you get it right.
GLOBAL MINDSET	You connect with people from all cultures and walks of life.
INFLUENCE	You get in the trenches to serve your community as an active leader.

RIPPLE IMPACT PLAN

VISION
What is your vision?

IDEA
What idea are you open to testing that will move you closer to your vision?

SWEET SPOT
Which one of your sweet spots is most aligned to your idea?

TEAM MEMBERS
What roles and talent do you need to execute your idea?

PARTNERS
What types of partners do you need or could collaborate with?

SOLIDARITY SQUAD
Who can you lean on from your close circle, your mentors, and your sponsors?

INSPIRED ACTIONS
How will you get into the trenches and take action in service of your vision?

IMPACT
What impact do you strive to make and how will you measure it?

FEEDBACK
How will you obtain feedback on your idea after you launch?

IDEA 2.0
As you test your idea, what other ideas or iterations of your original idea come to mind?

So what's next for you? Here are some suggestions:

1. Fill out your **Ripple Impact Plan**.
2. Go on a 100 Coffee Challenge (kudos to you if you started already). Access the **100 Coffee Challenge** Tool to help organize your strategy, meetings, and follow-ups.
3. If you're seeking to innovate within your organization, get the **Design Thinking Toolkit**.
4. Use the ***Innovation Starts With I* Digital Journal** to keep up the momentum built from reading this book with daily journal prompts.
5. Take a deeper dive to launch your next business idea by purchasing the ***Innovation Starts With I* Digital Workbook**.

You can access all these tools and resources at:

www.innovationstartswithi.com

And what's next for me? I already told you—stay tuned. And thank you so much for taking this journey with me. So far.

Follow me on LinkedIn, Instagram, Facebook, and Twitter:
@SaleemaVellani

Stay in touch through email updates:
www.saleemavellani.com

"WE'RE NEVER *singularly successful*. ESPECIALLY AS WE MOVE FORWARD AND THE WAY THE WORLD WORKS. **WE SHOULD EMBRACE ALLYSHIP.** ANY LEADER THAT CAN'T LEAD COLLABORATIVELY CAN'T BE A LEADER."
- COREY PONDER, FOUNDER OF EM|PACT STRATEGIES

"EVERYONE IS A CEO. EVERYTHING YOU DO EVERY DAY SHOULD BE A **LEARNING EXPERIENCE FOR YOUR OWN BUSINESS.** TRY AS MANY THINGS AS YOU POSSIBLY CAN."
– MIKE DUKE
FORMER CHIEF INNOVATION ARCHITECT, WELLS FARGO

"**ORGANIZATIONAL CULTURE** IS IMPORTANT SO THAT ALL EMPLOYEES ARE ENGAGED AND WANT TO COME TO WORK. EQUALLY IMPORTANT, THOUGH, IS **FOCUSING ON OUTCOMES**, SO THAT THE ORGANIZATION THRIVES AS MUCH AS EMPLOYEES."
– PATRICK VENNEBUSH, CHIEF LEARNING OFFICER, THE MATH LEARNING CENTER

"ASKING OURSELVES CHALLENGING QUESTIONS, AND BEING CRITICAL ABOUT HOW WE CAN **DO BETTER**, IS HOW WE WILL ENSURE THAT WE ARE ACTING FROM A PLACE OF **INTEGRITY** AND **AUTHENTICITY** IN ADDRESSING THE NEEDS OF COMMUNITIES ABOVE ALL ELSE."
– **ALIA ABAYA, COMMUNITY IMPACT DIRECTOR, ALTERNA SAVINGS**

"PURPOSE OVER PROFIT IMPLIES THESE THINGS ARE MUTUALLY **EXCLUSIVE** BUT ACTUALLY THESE THINGS CAN GO HAND IN HAND."
– **NICK DOMAN**, CO-FOUNDER + COO, OCEAN BOTTLE

"**INNOVATION** DISTINGUISHES BETWEEN A LEADER AND A FOLLOWER."
-STEVE JOBS

"**INVENTION** IS CONVERTING MONEY TO IDEAS. **INNOVATION** IS CONVERTING IDEAS INTO MONEY. EVERY ONE OF US PLAYS A CRITICAL ROLE IN INNOVATION. EXERCISE IT EVERY DAY TO KEEP YOURSELF RELEVANT."
– DR. JONATHAN REICHENTAL
AUTHOR, PROFESSOR AND FOUNDER

"**INNOVATION** BEGINS WITH YOUR UNIQUE POINT OF VIEW ON A PARTICULAR MARKET, IDENTIFYING **OPPORTUNITIES** BASED ON THAT UNIQUE PERSPECTIVE. FOLLOWING THIS, A COLLABORATIVE CO–INNOVATION APPROACH WITH YOUR CUSTOMER, YOUR TEAM AND YOUR PARTNERS ARE NEEDED IN AN ITERATIVE MANNER. OVERALL, INNOVATION MAY START WITH THE LETTER I BUT ALL THE OTHER PLAYERS OR LETTERS ARE NEEDED TO MAKE THE WORD A REALITY."
– IRFAN VERJEE, VICE PRESIDENT, SPRINKLR

Notes

INTRODUCTION

1. Feiler, Bruce. 2020. *Life Is In The Transitions. Mastering Change At Any Age.* Penguin Press.
2. "Fourth Industrial Revolution." World Economic Forum. Accessed May 22, 2021. https://www.weforum.org/focus/fourth-industrial-revolution

CHAPTER 1

3. Dorte Verner's photography focuses on people that have little voice and never make the news. She captures their beauty and strength through intimate moments. Dorte has received numerous awards for her photographs, including Nikon's Grand Prize and Most Popular Entry, winner of IPA, and Prix de la Photographie, Paris. Learn more at: https://www.dorteverner.com/
4. Verner, Dorte. "Is agriculture the way for refugees to rebuild their lives?" World Economic Forum. May 27, 2016. https://www.weforum.org/agenda/2016/05/is-agriculture-the-way-for-refugees-to-rebuild-their-lives/
5. Design thinking is a creative process for solving complex problems. According to Stanford University, where it started, the process involves five steps: Empathy, Define, Ideate, Prototype, and Test. It focuses on using empathy to really understand the problem you're trying to solve from different perspectives, especially from those you're designing the solution for.
6. Bhargava, Rohit. *Non Obvious Megatrends: How to See What Others Miss and Predict the Future.* Ideapress Publishing, 2020.
7. Benioff, Marc. TechCrunch Disrupt San Francisco Conference. 2013.

CHAPTER 2

8. Dubner, Stephen J. "Our Daily Bleg: Did I.B.M. Really See a World Market 'For About Five Computers'?" Freakonomics, April 17, 2008. https://freakonomics.com/2008/04/17/our-daily-bleg-did-ibm-really-see-a-world-market-for-about-five-computers/
9. Henry, Todd. *The Accidental Creative: How to Be Brilliant at a Moment's Notice*. Portfolio, 2011.
10. Adapted from Spiro, Rand J., John-Chang Jehng. 1990. "Cognitive flexibility and hypertext: Theory and technology for the non-linear and multi-dimensional traversal of complex subject matter." in *Cognition, education, and multimedia: Exploring ideas in high technology, ed. D. Nix & R.J Spiro* Lawrence Erlbaum Associates, Inc., 1990 (p. 163-205).
11. 'The Future of Jobs Report." World Economic Forum. October 2020. http://www3.weforum.org/docs/WEF_Future_of_Jobs_2020.pdf
12. Verner, Dorte, Saleema Vellani, Anne-Lise Klausen, and Edinaldo Tebaldi. *Frontier Agriculture for Improving Refugee Livelihoods: Unleashing Climate-Smart and Water-Saving Agriculture Technologies in MENA.* Washington, D.C. World Bank Group, 2017.
13. "H2Grow: Growing food in impossible places." World Food Programme. Accessed May 27, 2021. https://innovation.wfp.org/project/h2grow-hydroponics
14. Verner, Dorte, Nanna Roos, Afton Halloran, Glenn Surabian, Edinaldo Tebaldi, Maximillian Ashwill, Saleema Vellani, and Yasuo Konishi. *Insect and Hydroponic Farming In Africa: The New Circular Food Economy.* Washington, D.C. World Bank Group, 2021.

CHAPTER 3

15. "How to Identify Cognitive Bias." Masterclass. May 5, 2021. https://www.masterclass.com/articles/how-to-identify-cognitive-bias#what-is-cognitive-bias
16. Kahneman, Daniel. "Your Intuition Is Wrong, Unless These 3 Conditions Are Met." *ThinkAdvisor*. November 16, 2018. https://www.thinkadvisor.com/2018/11/16/daniel-kahneman-do-not-trust-your-intuition-even-for-stock-picking/

CHAPTER 4

17. Godin, Seth. *INBOUND*. 2020.

CHAPTER 5

18. The concept of Coopetition entered the business world in the late 1990s, pioneered by Harvard and Yale University professors Adam M. Brandenburger and Barry J. Nalebuf.
19. Bouquet, Cyril, Jean-Louis Barsoux, and Michael Wade. "Bring Your Breakthrough Ideas to Life How the most successful innovators do it." Harvard Business Review. December 2018.

CHAPTER 6

20. Wilson, Amy J. *Empathy for Change: How to Create a More Understanding World.* New Degree Press, 2021.
21. Already Always Listening™. Landmark Forum Syllabus: Day One. Landmark Worldwide. https://landmarkforumsyllabus.com/day-one/

CHAPTER 7

22. "The Consumer Content Report: Influence in the Digital Age." Stackla. Accessed May 27, 2021. https://stackla.com/resources/reports/the-consumer-content-report-influence-in-the-digital-age/

23. Association for Psychological Science. "Individualistic practices and values increasing around the world." ScienceDaily. www.sciencedaily.com/releases/2017/07/170718083800.htm Accessed July 9, 2020.
24. Storr, Will. *Selfie: How the West Became Self-Obsessed Author.* Pan Macmillan, 2017.
25. Bhargava, Rohit. *Non Obvious Megatrends: How to See What Others Miss and Predict the Future.* Ideapress Publishing, 2020.

CHAPTER 8

26. Psychology professor Albert Mehrabian at the University of California, Los Angeles, who laid out the concept in his book *Silent Messages* (1971).
27. Bye Bye Plastic Bags is a community engagement and educational movement driven by youth that advocates for no plastic bags. Learn more at: http://www.byebyeplasticbags.org/

CHAPTER 9

28. Tim Ferriss - Insights for Entrepreneurs - Amazon, January 29, 2018. https://www.youtube.com/watch?v=4T29mz6ymWM

CHAPTER 10

29. Caminhos Language Centre is the largest Portuguese language school in Rio de Janeiro, Brazil. The school supports Brazilian children and has a social program called Mais Caminhos. Learn more at: https://caminhoslanguages.com/

CHAPTER 11

30. Livermore, David A. *Cultural Intelligence (Youth, Family, and Culture): Improving Your CQ to Engage Our Multicultural World.* Baker Academic, 2009. p. 77.
31. Li, Ping et al. "Neuroplasticity as a function of second language learning: Anatomical changes in the human brain." *Cortex* 58 (2014): 301-324. https://sites.psu.edu/kaitlynlitcofsky/files/2017/02/Legault_Cortex_2014-pbpadj.pdf
32. "U.S. Businesses Need More Multilingual Employees." The Language Educator, Aug/Sept 2019. https://www.actfl.org/sites/default/files/tle/TLE_AugSept19_Article.pdf
33. "The Talent Shortage." Manpower Group. Accessed May 27, 2021. https://go.manpowergroup.com/talent-shortage-2018#thereport
34. Korn Ferry. "The global talent crunch: prepare for the impending talent shortage." 2020.

CHAPTER 12

35. "Business Formation Statistics." United States Census. Accessed May 27, 2021. https://www.census.gov/econ/bfs/index.html

Tools and Frameworks

Index

Book Team

SALEEMA VELLANI

AUTHOR | USA | @SALEEMAVELLANI

Saleema had a vision in 2014, and after a five-year hiatus, she transformed her story into this book. Her life mission is to serve entrepreneurs globally.

MICHAEL LEE

EDITOR | SOUTH AFRICA | @MICHAELLEECREATIVITY

Michael expanded Saleema's vision and brought the book's stories to life as a savvy storyteller and editor. His sweet spot is facilitating creative breakthroughs.

CATALINA CÔTAMO

CREATIVE DIRECTOR | COLOMBIA | @CATALINACOTAMO

Catalina managed the entire creative process of the book from day one. She is the Creative Director at Ripple Impact, a brand strategist, and a fashion designer.

SARA GOLISH

CREATIVE ADVISOR | CANADA | @SARAGOLISH

Sara drew the eye on the book cover and advised on the creative elements in the book. She is a visual artist, interior designer, and produces Islamic art.

SOFIE ENGSTORM VON ALTEN

BOOK ILLUSTRATOR | MEXICO | @HYPERKITSCH

Sofie transported readers around the world visually through producing the book illustrations. She runs a nonprofit artist residence in San Miguel de Allende.

MARÍA PAULA ZÚÑIGA ACUÑA

GRAPHIC DESIGNER | COLOMBIA

Maria Paula designed the tools sprinkled throughout the book and designed the digital workbook. She is also a professional make-up artist.

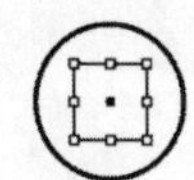

JUAN CAMILO CALDERÓN GONZÁLEZ

GRAPHIC DESIGNER | COLOMBIA

Juan helped conceptualize the book cover and contributed to the illustrations. He is also a UX / UI designer and photographer.

FAYYAZ VELLANI

WRITING ADVISOR | USA | @FAYYAZV

Fayyaz held Saleema accountable through cafe-hopping writing adventures and late night working sessions. He is a critical writing professor and musician.

Book Sponsors

A special thanks to all our sponsors
who helped bring this book to life.

JOIN THE JOURNEY JEFF FINKLE AL-NAWAZ & REHANA RAJAN
INTERNATIONAL ECONOMIC DEVELOPMENT COUNCIL
DR. FARAH ALANI | TO HEALTHY FEET PODIATRY AL-RIAZ ADATIA
NASSIB ELKADRI | USEREXPERIENCE.CA KEVIN MERCER | RAINGRID
THE THAROO FAMILY FUSION PRODUCTS LTD. LEILA JADIDI
SHAMINI DHANA | DHANA INC. TOW-R | TREAT OTHERS WITH RESPECT
HEBA RIZKANA | AZURILLION SOLUTIONS NABYL CHARANIA WORKTANGO
SHAMIM TEJPAR JAYMES CLONINGER TANJINA SHAPIRO
FAIZAL KASSAMALI JIM PEARSE EDI EXECUTIVE SEARCH | CONSULTING FIRM
NIZAR VELLANI FEIZEL SULEMAN DHD FILMS BASHIR & YASMIN
RIAZ & DINAR VELLANI ANTONIO IACOPINO
ZEENAT REMTULLA ASHRAF REMTULLA KICHOCHEO AIMAN KABLI
CANTON & COMPANY DR. GRANT ERHUANGA THE MUSAPHIR FAMILY
DC VISIONARIES INNOVAZING MAIKO UENO JOHN VELTKAMP
MARCO SEGURA MORALES SMART MENTOR | WWW.SMARTMENTOR.IO
SHELMINA BABAI ABJI ERIK HAVILAND WITH THEFUZE
ANAR & KARIM SAMJI AZMEENA SALEHANI NADIA & ALI CHUNARA
JENNIFER HART | INTELEKTULARO ADIL & KAI VELLANI MUMTAZ VELLANI

It means a lot to have your support. Thanks for
believing in our project and investing in our vision.

saleema vellani
+ Team

1. Adam Smiley Poswolsky, Generational Workforce Speaker and Author
2. Aiman Kabli, Author and Entrepreneur
3. Aisha Al-Kharusi, Global Business Leader
4. Alex Fernandez-Garita, Corporate Social Responsibility Leader, Johnson & Johnson
5. Alex Osterwalder, Creator of the Business Model Canvas
6. Alia Abaya, Community Impact Director, Alterna Savings
7. Ali Shakil, Associate Partner, IBM
8. Allison Wright, Organization Effectiveness Leader, Verizon
9. Alistair Brett, Chief Scientist
10. Ameena Bucheri, Co-Founder and CEO, Telp
11. Amy J. Wilson, Author and Empathy Leader
12. Anand Dass, Director, Platform Partnerships Workplace by Facebook
13. Andreina Marrón, Co-Founder and CEO, IVO Talents
14. Angela Specht, Vaccine Access Strategy and Impact Leader, Johnson & Johnson
15. Angie Wilen, Director of Strategic Transformation, Freddie Mac
16. Anita Nahal, Author, Professor and Diversity and Inclusion Leader
17. Annette Simmons, Author, The Story Factor
18. Arianna Huffington, Author and CEO, Thrive Global
19. Ashley Pallathra, Therapist and Author
20. Bayo Adelaja, CEO, Do It Now Now
21. Benjamin Atkinson, Innovation Engineer, Toyota
22. Benjamin Shapiro, Chief Scientist, Kernel
23. Bill O'Connor, Innovation Strategist
24. Bob Mosher, Chief Learning Evangelist, APPLY Synergies

25. Cate Luzio, Founder and CEO, Luminary
26. Chris Vestal, Change Management Leader, Washington Metropolitan Area Transit Authority
27. Christian Leitz, Head Corporate Responsibility, UBS
28. Corey Ponder, Founder, Em|Pact Strategies
29. Cristina Collazos, Startup Investment Program Manager, City of Knowledge
30. Daphne Leger, Innovation Strategist and Professor
31. Desmond P. Smith, Chief Customer Officer, Fannie Mae
32. Diego Noriega, Entrepreneur and Author
33. Diya Khanna, Global Diversity and Inclusion Leader, Amazon
34. Doug Galen, Co-Founder and CEO, Rippleworks Foundation
35. Eleni Pallas, Executive Coach and Organizational Activist
36. Ellie Bahrmasel, Co-Founder and CEO, Further Faster Design
37. Eric Koester, Georgetown Professor and Founder, The Creator Institute
38. Erica Young, Workplace Innovation Catalyst, Society for Human Resource Management
39. Eva-Marie Muller-Stuler, Chief Data Scientist, IBM
40. Gregg Brown, Author and Change Agent
41. Gustavo Araujo, Chief of Talent Acquisition, Organization for Security and Co-operation in Europe
42. Hariraj Vijayakumar, Founder and CEO, Designs In Change
43. Ian Calvert, Founder, FURTHER and Ex Global Project Leader, Red Bull Amaphiko
44. Ira Kaufman, Author and Digital Transformation Strategist
45. Irfan Verjee, Vice President, Sprinklr
46. Isaac Sacolick, Author, Driving Digital and President, StarCIO
47. Janet Roller, Head of Brand, Audience and Insights, Shutterfly
48. Jason Williams, Marketing and Innovation Strategist

49. Jeffrey Carpenter, Vice President of Innovation, Vantage Point
50. Jeremy Agnew, Social Entrepreneur
51. Jérôme Selva, Global Managing Director, Pegasystems
52. Jim Williams, Global Learning Advisor
53. Joe Hutsko, Writer and Technology Consultant
54. Jonathan Reichental, Author, Professor and Founder
55. Kamelia Hammachi, Business Development and Pedagogy Specialist, Kaizen Academy Algeria
56. Kasandra Moultrie, Diversity, Equity and Inclusion Leader, Google
57. Ken Wilson, Social Impact Researcher and Investor
58. Kimberly Coletti, Senior Director of Innovation, Save the Children
59. Kristy Wallace, CEO, Ellevate
60. Leon Wang, Biomimicry Professional
61. Lionel Bodin, Managing Director, Accenture Development Partnerships
62. Mark Horozowski, Founder and CEO, MovingWorlds
63. Maria Tafuri, Vice President of Global Sales, IBM
64. Michael Lee, Innovation Strategist
65. Mike Duke, Former Chief Innovation Architect, Wells Fargo
66. Mike Masserman, Former Head of Global Policy and Social Impact, Lyft
67. Mike Pino, Digital Learning and Technology Strategist
68. Monica H. Kang, Founder and CEO, InnovatorsBox
69. Neetal Parekh, Social Entrepreneur and Ecosystem Builder
70. Neil Kleinberg, Tech Entrepreneur and Professor
71. Nick Doman, Co-Founder and COO, Ocean Bottle
72. Nicole Motter, Chief Social Innovation Strategist
73. Nina Ansary, Author and Historian
74. Patrick Vennebush, Chief Learning Officer, The Math Learning Center
75. Pieter Spinder, Author and Entrepreneur
76. Rachel An, Human Resources and Innovation Leader

77. Rachel Hutchisson, Vice President, Corporate Citizenship and Philanthropy, Blackbaud
78. Rehana Nathoo, Founder and CEO, Spectrum Impact
79. Renato Azevedo Sant Anna, Digital Business Strategist and Innovation Advisor
80. Reuben Abootorabi, Founder and CEO, The Austin Agency
81. Robin Hirsch Everhart, SVP, Chief HR and Transformation Officer, LP Building Solutions
82. Rohit Bhargava, Trend Curator and Author
83. Rohit Sharma, Product Design Engineer
84. Sangram Vajre, Author and Co-founder, Terminus
85. Sara Ness, Founder, Authentic Revolution
86. Shalonda Ingram, Social Entrepreneur
87. Shamini Dhana, Social Entrepreneur
88. Sherika Ekpo, Global Diversity and Inclusion Lead, Google
89. Steve Blank, Creator, The Customer Development Method
90. Steve diFilipo, Chief Information Officer
91. Steven Rodriguez, Ecosystem Builder and Regional Manager, Techstars
92. Thos Gieskes, Managing Director, Oikocredit
93. Tom LaPlante, Chief Strategy Officer, Inspire.World
94. Torian Richardson, Global Diversity Recruiting Leader, NVIDIA
95. Tushar Hazra, Business and Technology Executive
96. Valentina Nesci, Diversity and Inclusion Leader and Career Coach, Google
97. Vanessa Van Edwards, Founder and CEO, Science of People
98. Yassi Dastan, Senior Director of Quality Engineering, Cvent
99. Zac Gittens, Business Strategist and Startup Mentor
100. Zahraa Dagher, Designer and Strategist

Acknowledgements

Sleepless nights, weekends lost, family time sacrificed, and many times, I felt like giving up. I couldn't have finished this book without my main Solidarity Squad—you.

My first and foremost thanks goes to my Mum. I know you would be proud of me. Even though we couldn't co-found a Montessori school together, we will spark curiosity among youth around the world. Dad, thanks for all your support and patience, ensuring I stayed committed, even if it meant sacrificing time together or you having to come along on my ad hoc visits to innovation hubs around the world. Adil, thanks for reminding me of who I am and all your big brother advice along the way. Fayyaz, thanks for teaching me not to judge myself when writing, always being down to go cafe-hopping and write together, and advising me every step of the way. Aman, thank you for always responding to my WhatsApps when I needed your input. Thank you to all of my extended family too.

A special thanks to all those who helped bring this book to life in many ways, especially Adam Smiley Poswolsky, Amy J. Wilson, Carmen Del Río Paracolls, Catherine Wood, Eric Koester, Gbenga Ogunjimi, Heather Ingram, Ira Kaufman, Monica Kang, Ricardo Abella, Shane Yeager, and Steven Rodriguez.

Thanks to all our partners and collaborators. Thank you Avner Landes, Chris O'Byrne, Celene Di Stasio, Craig Chavis Jr., Jaden Baum, Jonathan Mutch, Pearce Cacalda, Tariq Qureishy, and Tom Martin. The rest of you know who you are.

Thank you to our dream team at Ripple Impact. Catalina, words can't express the gratitude I have for you. Thank you for taking care of our Ripple Impact family and running the business operations so I could get this book done. Sean, thanks for holding me accountable no matter how many times I felt like giving up. Michael Lee, you are a master storyteller. You unfolded my story in ways I didn't know how to tell as well as the new story I'm about to live. Thank you Ana, Ashley, Carly, Clara, Christian, Diego, Diyaa, Hira, Jack, Juan, Maria Paula, Pam, Shayaan, Stiven, Vernée, and Zeenar for making my book journey a fun, colorful one.

A huge thank you to all our book sponsors from our Indiegogo campaign, listed on Page 277. You reached into your hearts and your pockets to support this book's publishing in the middle of a global pandemic. We wouldn't have gotten this far and wide without you.

Thanks to all the people I interviewed for this book, listed on Page 279. Your insights not only helped shape this book—they helped shape me. Thank you for making yourselves available for an exchange of ideas and sharing your collective thousands of years of experience.

A special thank you to these and other peer reviewers for your feedback on the drafts of the manuscript: Aman Vellani, Dr. Arnaud Cottet, Ashtar Boulos, Dan Rego, Fayyaz Vellani, Heather Ingram, Reuben Abootorabi, Sarah Gädig, Sara Golish, Shamini Dhana, Dr. Tulio Cravo, and Dr. Tushar Hazra.

Thanks to the communities that unleashed personal growth and supported my reinvention process and my author journey: Ripple Impact Community, Ismaili Professionals Network, TEDxTAMU, AHRMIO, World Bank Youth-2-Youth Community, WHO Innovators, SheCAN!, Ellevate, A Small World, StartingBloc, Author Support Group with Smiley, Creator Institute, University Startups, Women of Washington, SWANtrepreneurs, and STARS.

Thanks to my friends for being there for me on this wild ride, especially Amy, Azmeena, Jessica, Natasha, Rosemary, Saleheh, Sara, Sherry, and Tanjina. You showed up when I needed you most.

Thanks to my mentors, especially Bob Byrne, Dorte Verner, Ken Wilson, Mohamed Bhanji, Negar Rafikian, Patricia Froyo, and Paula Recimil Fuentes. Thank you to all my mentees and students over the years for helping shape my journey.

Thank you to all the hybridpreneurs and entrepreneurs in the Ripple Impact Community and Accelerators. Working with you has made my days brighter and inspired many insights in this book and outside of it.

Thank you to all the amazing women in my life. You have lifted me up.

BERRIKUNTZA
ІННОВАЦІЯ
नवीनता
ІНАВАЦЫЯ
NAUJOVĖ
NUÁLAÍOCHT
INNOVACIÓN
INNOVATIOUN
ARLOESEDD
ინოვაცია
ИНОВАЦИЈА
INNOVACIÓ ИНОВАЦИИ
INNOVATION INOVACE નવીનતા
innovation ИНОВАЦИЯ YNNOVAASJE
INOVACIJE INNUVAZIONE
NÝSKÖPUN 革新 INNOVÁCIÓ
INNOVATION
INOVACIJA innovatsioon
ИННОВАТСИОНӢ
INNOWASIÝA
INNOVAZZJONI
혁신 HAL-ABUURNIMO
ĐỔI MỚI חידוש حدث
YANGILIK INOVÁCIA INOVACIJA
INOVACIJA YENILIK ÙR-GHNÀTHACHADH
INNOVATIE ИНОВАЦИЯ
INOVAÇÃO
INOVAȚIE
INNOVAATIO
INNOVAZIONE INNOVATION
INNOWACJA INNOVACIÓN

About The Author

FOUNDER

Saleema Vellani is Founder and CEO of Ripple Impact, a business accelerator and community that helps entrepreneurs grow their companies and build their platforms. At the age of 21, Saleema co-founded and launched Brazil's top-rated language school, and at 22, she co-founded an online translation agency to help companies expand their digital presence globally. She has co-founded nine ventures with three exits.

INNOVATION STRATEGIST

Saleema has co-authored fifteen research studies published by the World Bank and the Inter-American Development Bank. In 2017, she co-led an award-winning study on addressing food insecurity in conflict-affected countries using climate-smart technologies, and is currently conducting groundbreaking research to promote a circular economy.

ADJUNCT PROFESSOR

Saleema is Adjunct Professor of Social Entrepreneurship at University Startups. She also teaches Design Thinking and Entrepreneurship at Johns Hopkins University and guest lectures at business schools. Saleema holds a BA from McGill University and an MA from Johns Hopkins University School of Advanced International Studies.

KEYNOTE SPEAKER

Saleema speaks on innovative leadership, entrepreneurship, and inclusive innovation. She gave a TEDx talk at Texas A&M University in March 2021.

AUTHOR

Saleema is the author of Innovation Starts With I. She contributes to Forbes and has been featured in Technically, Vox, ReWorked, and CMSWire.

@SaleemaVellani
saleemavellani.com
requests@rippleimpact.co

Made in the USA
Middletown, DE
09 March 2024

50582054R00177